TWAYNE'S WORLD AUTHORS SERIES

A Survey of the World's Literature

Sylvia E. Bowman, Indiana University
GENERAL EDITOR

FRANCE

EDITOR

Joseph de Maistre

TWAS 407

Joseph de Maistre

JOSEPH DE MAISTRE

By CHARLES M. LOMBARD

University of Illinois

TWAYNE PUBLISHERS

A DIVISION OF G. K. HALL & CO., BOSTON

Library of Congress Cataloging in Publication Data

Lombard, Charles M
  Joseph de Maistre.

  (Twayne's world authors series ; TWAS 407 : France)
  Bibliography: p. 153 - 54.
  Includes index.
  1. Maistre, Joseph Marie, comte de, 1753-1821.
PQ2342.M28Z69   808 [B]   76-13846
ISBN 0-8057-6247-7

Contents

About the Author

Charles M. Lombard is Professor of French at the University of Illinois. He has specialized in Franco-American literary relations during the Romantic period. His publications include *French Romanticism on the Frontier*, published by Editorial Gredos in Madrid and *Lamartine*, a volume in Twayne's World Authors Series. Lamartine was also the subject of Professor Lombard's doctoral dissertation at the University of Wisconsin. In addition, Professor Lombard has written several articles on Lamartine for learned journals.

Professor Lombard's current projects include a forthcoming Twayne United States Authors Series study of Thomas Holley Chivers, a controversial contemporary of Edgar Allan Poe and a World Authors study of Xavier de Maistre, Joseph de Maistre's younger brother who was a popular writer of the Romantic period.

Preface

While Joseph de Maistre has been the subject of books concerned primarily with his importance as a philosopher and political thinker, only limited attention has been given by scholars in France to his status as a literary figure. This is largely due to his reputation, to a certain extent unwarranted, as a religious fanatic, if not a bigot. Such notoriety has also restricted the amount of study in English devoted to Maistre, the man of letters, a fact that justifies the work at hand.

There is a need to concentrate on the literary significance of Maistre's writings with, of course, proper reference to his philosophical and political ideas in order to provide the reader with an adequate frame of reference. No attempt is made here to present a detailed stylistic analysis owing to limitations of space. Furthermore, although Maistre was an accomplished stylist his place in literary history is of greater interest to students of French literature.

Joseph de Maistre's best known work, the *Soirées de Saint-Pétersbourg* is analyzed in some detail since this was deemed his major contribution to letters by contemporaries and posthumous admirers. Minor writings are also considered, with the aim of revealing his literary opinions on French and foreign writers. Emphasis is placed on both his Classical and Romantic leanings to clarify his role as precursor in a period of transition. Maistre's fondness for the paradox becomes apparent after a study of his works and serves to demonstrate his creative genius at its best. The vigor and energy with which Maistre wrote and expressed himself in striking symbols are illustrated by characteristic passages, thus enabling the reader to understand more clearly why Maistre appealed to a wide range of writers of varying temperaments. His correspondence is treated as well to disclose intimate aspects of this controversial writer and to give a more complete picture of his inner life and secret longings and aspirations.

Quotations are frequent and at times longer than usual, especially since there is no English translation of Maistre's complete works. It is hoped that this study will present in sharper perspective Maistre's place in French literature as one of the last noteworthy writers of the Classical epoch as well as the important part he played in the pre-Romantic movement.

CHARLES M. LOMBARD

University of Illinois

Chronology

1807   October, writes *Mémoire* to Savary on proposed interview with Napoleon.

1809   Maistre begins work on *Essai sur le principe générateur des constitutions politiques et des autres institutions humaines* and the *Soirées de Saint-Pétersbourg*. December 1, Maistre writes the *Lettre à une dame protestante*.

1810   February, Maistre composes the *Lettre à une dame russe*, popular with Russian ladies attracted to Catholicism. Writes the *Éclaircissements sur les sacrifices*. June-July, Maistre writes to Count Razoumovski the *Cinq lettres sur l'éducation publique en Russie*.

1811   September, Maistre composes for Count Razoumovski the *Mémoire sur la liberté de l'enseignement public*.

1814   Maistre writes *Te Deum*, intended as sermon in honor of restoration of king of Sardinia.

1815   June-September, Maistre writes the *Lettres sur l'inquisition espagnole* published in Paris in 1822. Maistre's wife and two daughters arrive at Saint Petersburg.

1817   May 27, Maistre leaves Russia with his family. June 24, Maistre and family arrive in Paris. July 7 and 8, Maistre visits Louis XVIII. During stay in Paris Maistre seeks Chateaubriand's aid in finding a publisher for *Du Pape*.

1819   December, *Du Pape* published in Lyons.

1821   February 26, death of Joseph de Maistre at Chambéry. July, publication of the *Soirées de Saint-Pétersbourg*. Publication of the *Éclaircissement sur les sacrifices*.

CHAPTER 1

Biographical Sketch and Early Works

I Early Years and First Stage of Career

JOSEPH de Maistre was born on April 1, 1753, in Chambéry, located in the province of Savoy which at that time constituted the French-speaking portion of the Italian kingdom of Sardinia. The government was reasonably progressive and had liberated the serfs in 1762. Maistre's father, a member of the senate of Savoy, had married at the age of forty-four the daughter of a judge, Christine Desmotz, his junior by seventeen years. Maistre was the third of fifteen children, five of whom died at an early age. A younger brother, Xavier, also became a writer.[1]

Joseph was first trained by Jesuit tutors and then studied at the royal college in Chambéry. When fifteen he joined the Confrérie des Pénitents Noirs, a religious group caring for condemned prisoners. In 1769 he went to Turin to study law and in 1773 began his association with the Freemasons, a group very much in vogue among fashionable young men. Along with others he formed a Scottish Rite lodge at Chambéry in 1778. His official Masonic title was "Joseph à Floribus" and he soon became a leader in his lodge. Concerned about the future of Freemasons in Europe he wrote a tract on the subject to the Masonic Grandmaster, the Duke of Brunswick. In the early 1780s Maistre visited Lyons and there was initiated into the esoteric teachings of Martinez-Pasqualis whose mystical formulas had great influence on those segments of Masonry adhering to theosophy.

After completing his law studies in Turin, Maistre entered into practice and read extensively in philosophy, history, and theosophy, especially the works of Louis-Claude de Saint-Martin, the self-styled "unknown philosopher." At first Maistre's career promised to be a modest one and he was beset with financial problems. He became a magistrate in 1772 and carried out his duties conscientiously.

11

When thirty-three Joseph married Françoise-Marguerite de Moraud by whom he had three children. His father died in 1789 and Maistre inherited the title of Count along with the task of supervising the estate and attending to the needs of his brothers and sisters. 1789 also marked the beginning of the French Revolution and three years later the ragged army of proletarian France swarmed over Sardinia. Maistre fled to Lausanne and took charge of diplomatic affairs in Switzerland for the Sardinian government. Although stripped of his property in Savoy Maistre thrived in the cultural ambiance of Lausanne. He now began to write in earnest and in addition to miscellaneous essays completed the *Considérations sur la France* in 1797 through which his name became known to émigré groups throughout Europe.

II *Residence at Russian Court*

In 1799 he was made regent of the island of Sardinia and in 1802 was appointed Sardinian ambassador to Russia. With a heavy heart he bade farewell to his family and set out for Saint Petersburg. Meager funds kept him from taking along his wife and children. Thus began a sojourn of fourteen years in Russia, the most important period in the life of Joseph de Maistre. During that time he had many rewarding contacts and associations and wrote his major works. While forced to live almost penuriously and grieved by the separation from loved ones he enjoyed, nevertheless, the diplomatic society at the Russian court. For a long time he was on cordial terms with the Czar.

A close friend of Maistre during his residence in Russia was Mme Anne Sophie Swetchine. She was born in Moscow on November 22, 1782. Her father, M. Soymonov, held an important position in the imperial government. Reared in the shadow of the Court of Catherine the Great she witnessed the splendor of the Empress' reign and received an excellent education in languages and philosophy. From the time of their first meeting Mme Swetchine was impressed by Maistre's wit and intellect. Soon he became her spiritual guide and began the long and difficult task of converting Mme Swetchine, a devout adherent of the Russian Orthodox faith, to Catholicism. She was deeply affected by the knowledge of the Count's poverty. Maistre often had only bread and water for breakfast even though obliged to maintain a footman and carriage essential to the outer dignity of an ambassador. In private conversation she usually found Maistre rather light and spontaneous in contrast to the measured intellectual tone of his writings. Whenever the Count was in a somber mood Mme Swetchine talked about his favorite subjects, philosophy and ancient languages, and even began an argument to oblige Maistre to forget his troubles and engage in a lively conversation. When she finally entered the Catholic Church in 1815 her motives for conversion were based as much on emotional factors as on theological reasoning. Maistre was delighted by her decision in which he played no small part. After Maistre's departure from Russia they continued to correspond. Mme Swetchine left Russia in 1816 to reside in Paris and attracted to her salon celebrities like Lacordaire, Montalembert, and Alexis de Tocqueville. Saddened by news of Maistre's death in 1821 she treasured the memory of their friendship. Mme Swetchine died in Paris in 1857.[2]

Thanks to his Masonic and theosophic background Maistre was at home with the illuminist clique in Saint Petersburg. He accepted that phase of illuminism in accord with his own interpretation of the theosophy of Saint-Martin. The Count's mystic vision of the future course of events in Europe and his own particular role led him to seek a personal interview with Napoleon. Maistre probably hoped to persuade Bonaparte to restore the Bourbons to the throne. When this failed he made overtures to Louis XVIII in order to become the exiled monarch's ambassador in Russia and suffered a second setback. Undismayed, Maistre continued to support the Bourbon cause.

Separation from his family, the source of many painful hours of loneliness, was mitigated by the presence in Russia of his brother, Xavier, and his son, Rodolphe. Through the Count's influence they both received appointments from the Czar. Finally, in 1815, after twelve years Maistre was joined in Russia by his wife and two daughters.

An interesting sidelight of Maistre's residence in Saint Petersburg was the information he discovered there about Charles XI, the unhappy king of Sweden. A believer in the most extravagant claims of illuminism as a key to the supernatural, in December, 1687, Charles XI was terrified by a horrendous hallucination. The details are mentioned in Maistre's correspondence. Later Mérimée was to use this incident as the story line of the *Vision de Charles XI*.

Among Maistre's close friends at Saint-Petersburg were a Russian senator, Basile Tamara, Count Blacas, a French émigré, and the Bavarian Ambassador to Russia, Graf François Gabriel de Bray. Maistre was always on warm terms with these three gentlemen and they supported his concerns at the Russian court. They were to become immortalized in the pages of the *Soirées de Saint-Pétersbourg*, a summary of Maistre's personal philosophy developed during his stay in Russia.

Czar Alexander, at first well disposed toward Maistre, kindled the latter's hopes of becoming mentor to the ruler of the largest empire in Europe. Subsequent distrust of Jesuit proselytism and suspicion of Maistre's connection with the conversion of Mme Swetchine and other prominent Russians to Catholicism put an end to the Count's dreams. The Czar did not agree with Maistre's vision of Russia's reunion with Rome and a Christian millenium in which the crowned heads of Europe would be united under the Pope.

III   *Departure from Russia and Last Years*

Caught up in the bitter resentment against the Jesuits and Catholics Maistre was obliged to leave Russia with his family on May 27, 1817. On his way back to Sardinia he visited France and saw Paris for the first time on June 24, 1817. While there he met Louis XVIII and found the king's manner rather cool. The royal displeasure may have been incurred by political opinions expressed in the *Essai sur le principe générateur des Constitutions*. Louis XVIII fancied himself a constitutional monarch and not an absolute ruler.

By this time Maistre was used to royal rebuffs and spent most of his time in Paris trying to win support for the publication of *Du Pape*. He first approached Chateaubriand who was too busy to help and then turned to Catholic scholars at Lyons who edited and corrected the manuscript. *Du Pape* was published in December of 1819.

Back home in Savoy after many years he received distinguished guests at his home, among them Lamartine, a promising writer of the young Romantic generation. A family bond was formed between the two writers when Lamartine's sister, Césarine, married Maistre's nephew, Count de Vignet. Despite some arguments to the contrary recent scholarship has proven convincingly that Joseph de Maistre was present at Lamartine's marriage to an English lady, Marianne Birch, and also signed the wedding contract.

The robust constitution that enabled Maistre to survive the Russian winters at last showed the effects of a hectic career. Joseph de Maistre died on February 26, 1821. His family compared his last moments to those of a saint, a view accepted by strict Catholics who idolized the Count. Even his opponents, and there were many, admired his rigid adherence to his principles and the sparkling wit, irony, and imagination revealed in his writings. Few could have foreseen the diverse and highly individualistic group of writers to be influenced by Joseph de Maistre.

IV Éloge de Victor-Amédée

When the King of Sardinia visited Savoy in 1775 Maistre, in honor of the occasion, penned the *Éloge de Victor-Amédée*. He had several copies printed at Lyons which were distributed to a few of his close friends, but there was no general publication of the work. Written in the lofty and rather bombastic style of the period, the *Éloge* prefigures only in a rather vague fashion the vigorous and energetic stylist of the *Soirées*.[3]

The *Éloge* evinces a tendency to compose individual phrases and sentences with a maximlike quality. Sentences like "Praise is a crime when one prostitutes it to vice" and "ambition, self-interest, pride, voluptuousness, all the vices crowd together on the steps of the throne"[4] demonstrate the author's penchant for moralizing as well as his concern for the integrity of the royal house of Sardinia.

Sensing a change in the traditional order of things Maistre fears an upheaval in the near future: "I tremble when I see that the bonds of society are beginning to be relaxed among us." Harbingers of catastrophe are discernible in the conduct of those kings *"who begin to reflect only* when the cry of the people announces that all is lost."[5] This latter observation might well have been intended to describe the current situation in France.

Maistre does not seem aware of the overly ideal picture he presents of the Sardinian monarch's paternal relations with his subjects. His description of the role of religion in the realm and the king's dependence on the Church seems borrowed from Bossuet: "She is the one who teaches him that his subjects are *his brothers;* she is the one who shows him beyond death a formidable judge who will cast in the same scale the monarch and the shepherd. . . ."[6]

While Maistre throughout the *Éloge* appears as an eloquent propagandist in the service of Victor-Amédée he is realistic in assessing the qualifications of the average king. The divine right to rule, Maistre recognizes, does not guarantee this privilege will be exercised by demigods: "What is a king? He's a man to whom Heaven has not given an intellect superior to that of an ordinary person and who has duties a thousand times more important to fulfill. . . ."[7]

At one juncture Maistre reveals that the Enlightenment affected even an ardent royalist and orthodox Catholic. In no uncertain terms he advises Victor Amédée to forget the bygone era of medievalism and concentrate instead on the role outlined for the progressive ruler by the political theorists of the eighteenth century: "Gothic institutions are going to disappear. Victor will lead true philosophy by the hand; he will order it to suffuse the old formulas; and ignorance, pursued, hunted, insulted throughout all Europe, will no longer brag that we are its last subjects."[8]

The extent to which the Enlightenment exercised any influence over Maistre was of course limited. Most likely he was shrewd enough to see that the *philosophes* had a point in clamoring for reform and deemed it prudent to act quickly before it was too late. Such a concern on Maistre's part would throw considerable light on the underlying *raison d'être* of the obvious toadyism in the *Éloge*. Lavish praise of the king would put him in the proper mood to heed the occasional words of sound advice offered by Maistre.

V   Discours sur la vertu

The *Éloge de Victor-Amédée III* established Maistre's reputation as a writer, and he was called upon two years later, in 1777, to give an address to fellow members of the juridical profession. At that time Maistre was a magistrate. The title of his oration was *Discours sur la vertu;* it remained in manuscript and was not published in full. In general the style of this second literary effort was characterized by the same ornate and highflowing phraseology used in the *Éloge*.

Despite a firm insistence that "Virtue is a constant force, an habitual state of the soul, completely independent of circumstances,"[9] Maistre could not treat a worn-out subject without becoming ensnared in the banalities accumulated by previous orators down through the ages. In one passage, however, Maistre again shows the results of his reading of the rationalists by echoing sentiments of a strongly Rousseauistic flavor. The young magistrate at one point in his oration underlines the significance of the general will in the formation of a commonwealth:

Picture to yourselves the birth of society; see these men, weary of the power of doing everything, gathered together in a throng around the sacred altars of the fatherland which has just been born; all abdicate voluntarily a part of their liberty; all consent to have individual wills bow under the scepter of the general will: the social hierarchy is going to be formed. . . .[10]

Maistre of course was incapable of adhering in any great measure to Rousseau's theory of the general will and while he seems momentarily to succumb to the notion of men in a distant period of history surrendering part of their liberty to a ruler, there are no grounds whatsoever for assuming he temporarily entertained a democratic concept of the origin of government. On the contrary, Maistre utilized Rousseau's description of the beginning of social inequality among men to depict the process by which mankind at an early stage recognized God's plan to have one ruler or king to exercise the powers of government. As Maistre specifically points out, a class system was organized as part of this early commonwealth.

VI   La Franc-Maçonnerie, Mémoire au duc de Brunswick

At the age of twenty-one Maistre became a member of the "Trois Mortiers," the local Masonic lodge, in 1774. Four years later he was the leading spirit in the establishment of a reformed Scottish Rite lodge, named "Parfaite Sincerité," in Chambéry. His Masonic name was "Joseph à Floribus" and he possessed in addition a number of impressive titles in recognition of his leadership in the society. The Church had not yet anathematized Freemasonry and Maistre was typical of the orthodox Catholics who, without compunction, joined its ranks. There were, in fact, two divergent groups in the order, one rationalist and antimonarchist and the other Christian and royalist.

In his association with the Masons, Maistre became acquainted at Lyons with the esoteric ideas of a certain Martinez-Pasqualis whose origins and background are veiled in mystery. When Maistre was in the process of being initiated into the arcana of Martinez's teaching he also had contact with the illuminism of Louis-Claude de Saint-Martin. The latter's *L'Homme de désir* was to have considerable influence on the *Soirées de Saint-Pétersbourg*. Maistre always defended the sincerity of Saint-Martin whom he considered an orthodox thinker and a sublime mystic.

During the French Revolution, Sardinian Freemasons were suspected of seditious activities. To satisfy the king Maistre voluntarily suspended the meetings of his lodge but continued to study the literature of Freemasonry and the theosophy of Saint-Martin. While in Russia, in 1810, he was invited to join a lodge in Saint-Petersburg but refused, since he was aware of the Czar's anti-Masonic sentiments.

The *Mémoire au duc de Brunswick* was finished at Chambéry on

June 15, 1782. It remained unpublished until 1925 when Emile
Dermenghem had a critical edition printed by Rieder in Paris.
Savaron, a member of Maistre's lodge, took the *Mémoire* to a
Masonic council at Wilhelmsbad where he represented the
Freemasons of Chambéry. Maistre's commentary was delivered to
the Grandmaster, Duke Ferdinand de Brunswick-Lunebourg. With
a view to restoring order in European Freemasonry, beset with conflicting beliefs and practices, the duke called the council in the hope
of achieving unity. The main question to be discussed was the role of
occultism in the society. Although the illuminists triumphed over the
rationalists, Maistre considered the outcome a pyrrhic victory
because, in his estimation, the voice of the Holy Spirit was not
heeded in the proceedings.[11]

Those Catholics who were Freemasons generally felt themselves
superior to the average Catholic by reason of the higher realm of
mystical truths into which they were initiated, thanks to their
membership in the society. From their standpoint the great mass of
Catholics constituted a lower degree or blue lodge, in Masonic terminology, and were thus incapable of a more refined religious experience. Maistre shared this opinion, a fact that explains his own
unique position in entertaining some rather odd notions derived
from theosophy while claiming all the time to be a practicing
Catholic.

Maistre wastes no words in informing the Duke of Brunswick that
many Masonic customs, such as passwords, seem rather silly, as do
also the extravagant claims of tracing the order's origins to the
destruction of the Templars. In modern times Masons would do well,
Maistre sternly advises, to concern themselves with the religious
enlightenment of mankind. The Templar ideal of the monk-soldier
patently has no place in the eighteenth century. More relevant is the
question of a primitive revelation of man's full and ultimate
regeneration. When the sages of early civilizations spoke of this
primitive revelation they had in mind two interpretations, one for
the masses and another, more esoteric and profound, for the
privileged few.

New candidates should not be forced to accept the teachings of
Freemasonry all at once, Maistre tells the Grandmaster. The principles promulgated by the order had of necessity to be those
preached by the Catholic Church, the sole repository of divine
revelations in the fullest sense. In accomplishing this, Masonry must
perforce purge itself of rationalism and perverse brands of il-

luminism. Maistre has in mind the *philosophes* and the anti-Catholic phase of illuminism in Germany.

In the reforms proposed by Maistre to the Grandmaster the first on the list is the reunion of all the Christian Churches. A good starting point was a symposium of Catholics and Lutherans centered around the Augsburg Confession, a document which, Maistre insists, shows the two groups have much in common. The proper interpretation of Scripture would be essential to the task of reunion. Here Maistre recommends careful attention to both the literal and allegorical meaning of the Bible, keeping in mind that early Christians were very sensitive to the figurative sense of many passages in Scripture.

Stressing the need for internal reform in Masonic lodges Maistre outlines in some detail the qualifications for the various degrees in the order. The oath of membership would be simple and direct, commit members to honorable deeds, and contain nothing against religion and country. Rules of Masonry would of course be in French, the clearest and most logical language to Maistre's way of thinking. Last of all, Masons everywhere would do well to pattern their governmental structure after the Holy See in Rome.

Maistre wrote the *Mémoire* when he was twenty-nine and with a young man's proclivity to play the iconoclast. The fuzzy notions of some Masons on the subject of occultism leave Maistre singularly unsympathetic: "There would be innumerable things to say about the nature of true allegories, and about the excess of illogic in which writers otherwise highly respected have seen themselves carried away by the mad passion of seeking and explaining mysteries. . . ."[12]

Freemasonry as interpreted by some was originally a vulgar institution, Maistre suggests, representing "a detached and perhaps corrupt branch of an ancient respectable stem."[13] Not inclined at this early period of his development to idealize the past, Maistre blithely ridicules the cherished idols of older Masons with the incisiveness of a Voltaire attacking Catholicism. The entire structure of the order is in need of thorough reform, Maistre maintains, and no precept of Freemasonry is too sacrosanct to escape the demands of sensible change: "Can't one be useful and virtuous without precursors? We are all united in the name of religion and humanity. We can answer for the integrity of our intentions. Let us boldly take the edifice by the foundations and, instead of renewing, let us create!"[14]

Maistre is eager to be the iconoclast when cleansing Masonry of false superstitions and myths, but he assumes a different attitude when the primitive revelation of transcendent truths is at stake. Then he adopts a more serious and dogmatic tone: "As, according to Pascal's remark, false miracles prove the true ones, in like manner the abuse of allegorical explanations announces that this doctrine had a real foundation which we have lost sight of."[15]

In any analysis of the *Mémoire* it is important to bear in mind that Maistre was addressing the Duke of Brunswick, a Lutheran. Accordingly, he is somewhat circumspect in broaching the subject of Catholicism. He suggests that Catholics and Lutherans are the logical parties to commence any ecumenical dialogue. This proposal, together with the call to unite Masons under the banner of Christianity against rationalism and heretical illuminism, was calculated to please the duke. Nowhere, however, is there any indication that Maistre speaks primarily as a Mason relegating Catholicism to secondary consideration. An indifferent Catholic would not ask for a reorganization of Masonic administration along papal lines. The oath in defense of God and country which Maistre demands of Masons is unquestionably intended mainly for Catholic lodges, although it would apply incidentally to Lutheran groups as well.

Nothing could be further from the truth than to use the *Mémoire* to prove Maistre was at this period skeptical in matters of religion and even anticlerical. At the very moment he was espousing Freemasonry he also belonged to a group of laymen who had periodic retreats under the guidance of Jesuits. Both facts must be kept in view in any study of Maistre at this critical stage of his development.

Besides the temptation to seek out evidence in the *Mémoire* of Maistre's indifference to the Church there is also the tendency to conclude that this early treatise contains the main ideas Maistre was to develop more fully later in the *Soirées*. While the Count makes passing reference to the first fall and man's regeneration as truths disclosed in a primitive revelation at the dawn of civilization, no mention is made of important concepts subsequently discussed in the *Soirées* and in other works. In the *Mémoire* there is actually little to indicate Maistre would become a polemical writer displaying impressive literary powers. With the exception of a discernible penchant for irrationalism and a striking clarity in the expression of ideas, there is little to show that the author of the communication to the Duke of Brunswick was to become a noteworthy forerunner of Romanticism.

CHAPTER 2

First Major Works

I Considérations sur la France

AFTER fleeing the invasion of Savoy by a French revolutionary army in September, 1792, Maistre returned briefly to Chambéry in November. Unable to live under and pay taxes to the new regime in Savoy he departed for Switzerland. The persecution of the Church and hounding of the priests were more than he could bear.

During his sojourn in Lausanne from 1793 to 1797 Maistre remained in the service of the Sardinian king and, through a spying operation he helped to organize, gathered for the monarch intelligence data from French-occupied Savoy. Owing to financial straits he was obliged to live in a very modest fashion on a limited income. Popular in the émigré salons in Lausanne, he tried to help exiles with friends and families still living in France. During this period he wrote the *Considérations sur la France*, published in 1796.

Maistre's work was heartily applauded in émigré circles; its prediction of a rosy future when aristocracy would be restored and its hard-nosed analysis of the current state of affairs from a conservative standpoint raised the hopes of a select but influential minority temporarily displaced by the Revolution and by Napoleon.

The provocative opening statement of the *Considérations* is clearly a direct reply to Rousseau's dictum that everywhere man is in chains. In an explicit denial of this slogan Maistre stresses the gentle bonds that tie men to legitimate authority: "We are attached to the throne of the Supreme Being by a supple chain which holds us without enslaving us."[1] This felicitous relationship in normal times assures society a happy existence: "But in times of revolutions the chain which binds man is shortened abruptly . . . carried along by an unknown force he rebels against it and instead of kissing the hand which clasps him he insults it or refuses to recognize it."[2]

Recalling recent events in France Maistre singles out Mirabeau as a protagonist in the drama that unfolded in the early days of the Revolution. "At bottom he was the *king of the market-place*. By the crimes he committed . . . he helped the popular movement."[3]

The sanguinary scenes of the Terror were of such magnitude that historians had to tax their brains to remember when bloodshed of this nature had occurred previously in French history. A few innocent people, Maistre concedes, may have died but a terrible punishment was inflicted on a great number of guilty parties. To Maistre's mind the words of Hamlet in Act III, Scene 8, describing a frightful pit into which people flung themselves, aptly depicted the terrifying events of the Revolution.

Countless questions have been raised concerning the cause and possible explanation of the Terror, observes Maistre, but no one really knew the answer except God. Once the Revolution was in full swing and Louis XVI deposed, only the Jacobins had the power to rectify the situation. The solution they found was a dreadful one indeed, but the outcome could be predicted given the character of the Jacobins' bloodthirsty leader: "The infernal genius of Robespierre alone could effect this wonder. The revolutionary government hardened the soul of the French by soaking it in blood."[4] By this gruesome operation on the minds and hearts of the people France acquired the stamina to survive the Terror and the coalitions of the European powers. Only the return of the Bourbons would bring the desired change. When this happened "The black magic which is in operation at this moment would disappear like a fog bank before the sun."[5]

The blame was not entirely on the side of the Jacobins and other revolutionary leaders in the opinion of Maistre. He was quick to point out the shortcomings of the clergy who failed to live up to their duties as representatives of the Church. Wealth, luxury, and an easygoing life-style stifled the spirit that glorified Christian France in the seventeenth century.

To Maistre the conclusion was inescapable: blood baths marked almost every period of history and seemed an inevitable consequence of the human condition. The current situation in France had its counterparts in various periods of mankind's development. To illustrate this point Maistre gives a panoramic view of war as it plagued humanity throughout history:

I will not pursue this terrible picture further; our century and the one that preceded it are too well known. If one goes back to the cradle of nations; if one comes down to our times; if one examines people in all possible situations, from the state of barbarism to that of the most refined society, one will find war. . . .[6]

Turning to the fine arts for which he had great admiration, Maistre refuses to admit that they thrive only on peace. As far back as ancient Greece Euripides has Apollo explain to Orestes that war is an atonement for the sins of man against the gods. Art flourishes in time of war or peace and draws themes from these two sets of circumstances so common to humanity. In modern times the palingenesis of a Charles Bonnet, like that of Saint Paul, traced vividly the return of society to life after apparent death. The French Revolution did not hinder the capacity of the human spirit, for aesthetic expression could thrive even under the most dire conditions. "The observers of great human calamities are led especially to these sad meditations."[7]

Pursuing the theme of catastrophes foisted upon society Maistre notes that carnage in its worst form occurs among large populations. Much of this manifestation of brutality transpires under a republic, an evil thing in itself since it contradicts the divine will. Evil however, the words of Rousseau notwithstanding, is to Maistre only a negative concept and merely denotes the absence of a positive quality. Rousseau's theory of the general will of the people is an example of evil and is a patent distortion of the divine plan of government.

"There is in the French Revolution," Maistre reflects, "a satanic character which distinguishes it from all that has been seen and perhaps all that will be seen."[8] In a whimsical vein — and as a further exploration of the diabolical aspects of the Revolution — Maistre imagines himself seated at the National Convention and like Shakespeare, "the sublime bard of England," transported into another world: "I see the enemy of mankind sitting at the merry-go-round and convoking all the *evil spirits* in this new Pandemonium."[9]

From this apocalyptic vision of the crisis in France Maistre passes to the more urgent question of the future of the Church: "Either a new religion is going to be formed or Christianity will be revitalized in some extraordinary manner."[10] The cult of Reason under Robespierre can only be a passing fancy. It is a fundamental tenet of natural law that a legitimate state or order will be restored in the baptism of blood occasioned by the Terror. Robespierre is in charge at the moment and in some strange way seems to carry out God's will.

English influence in moderation is viewed by Maistre as a salutary factor but, exaggerated beyond all sensible proportions, it leads to the excesses of the French Revolution. Charles I was dealt with equitably and under the unwritten traditions of English law. A gross manipulation of the facts caused the revolutionists in France to cite the English experience as a justification for the bloody turmoil that started in 1789. Even in the realm of *belles lettres* this anglomania prevailed. Maistre, in spite of his fondness for Shakespeare, rejects the contention of some French critics that the English dramatist is superior to Racine.

Abandoning the tone of the professional philosopher Maistre lapses momentarily into a Pascalian mood: "But what are we, weak and blind humans! and what is this trembling light that we call *Reason*?"[11] Whereas Pascal told readers to listen to the heart and seek God through simple, religious faith, Maistre instructs readers to put aside aimless reasoning in political matters and to have greater reliance on the form of government authorized by God, namely, monarchy. "Rid yourself for once of these destructive doctrines," he pleads, "which have dishonored our century and doomed France."[12] Just as true peace and tranquility are found in the spiritual life through conformity to God's designs, Maistre seems to argue, so are peace and harmony assured in the political sphere through acceptance of monarchy, the form of government the Lord has intended for men. There are practical considerations as well: "If one envisages the question under a more general point of view, one will find that monarchy is, without contradiction, the government which gives the most distinction to a greater number of persons."[13]

With an obvious borrowing from Montesquieu's principle of the necessity for honor and recognition under a monarchy Maistre praises the nobility of the *ancien régime*. In general many aristocrats proved the adage that good blood will inevitably assert itself. Not all of the nobles were perfect and the worst were turncoats who joined the Revolution. In addition, the flight of the nobility from the country deprived France of its traditional leadership. Here Maistre prefigures the theme of Vigny's *Cinq-Mars* that Louis XIII's fatal mistake was the failure to accept the great nobles as partners in government instead of making them completely subservient to the Crown, a step that stripped them of their virility and desire to support France in time of need. Like Vigny in *Cinq-Mars* Maistre describes poignantly the insidious effect of the French Revolution on the monarchy: "The red bonnet, by touching the royal forehead, caused the traces of the holy oil to disappear; the charm is broken."[14]

Disgusted with the French Revolution, Maistre took delight in drawing embarrassing parallels between it and the revolt against Charles I, which occurred within a legitimate framework provided by unwritten law and not by an artificial man-made constitution. The roots of the grievances of the English rebels were deeper than those of the French revolutionaries: "The fanaticism of liberty, inflamed by that of religion, penetrated souls much more profoundly than it did in France where the cult of liberty rests on nothingness."[15]

The horrible situation in which the French nation found itself in the 1790s can ultimately be explained by viewing its plight in light of the plans of Providence. Maistre frequently discards the methodology of a systematic philosophy in an endeavor to acquire almost clairvoyant insights into the underlying reasons for the Terror. Why did God permit it? "In truth, one would be tempted to believe that political revolution is only a secondary object of the great plan which is unfolded before us with a terrible majesty."[16]

If France is to resume one day her leadership in Europe it must have a second baptism of blood, for God has allowed in His wisdom certain evils to exist. No nation can escape indefinitely the consequences of its membership in a society marked by violence. "Human blood must flow without interruption on the globe . . . peace for each nation is only a respite."[17]

It is possible to try to educate sovereigns in the ways of peace, but any such approach must be made with circumspection. Sane men should avoid the temptation of entertaining the dreams of Condorcet and his absurd notion of human perfectibility. The causes of disorder had to be checked and nipped in the bud. This is no easy task since even in Homer's great epic on the Trojan war the spilling of blood was judged necessary to atone for the sins of mortals, even if it meant that innocent persons must suffer. Little more can be expected: "There is only violence in the universe; but we are spoiled by modern philosophy, which has said that *all is well*, whereas evil has sullied everything, and in a very real sense, *all is evil*, because nothing is in its place. . . ."[18]

Strife characterizes all phases of life and even the world of ideas is not exempt. Maistre reminds readers that since the Enlightenment two opposing schools of thought have battled for control of the European mind: "The present generation is witness to one of the greatest spectacles . . . the struggle of Christianity and philosophism."[19] In anticipating a continuation of this debate, Maistre underscores the significance of this intellectual conflict, praises the role of

Christianity in European history, and forecasts the downfall of eighteenth-century rationalism through its inherent errors. If Christianity, the "Christian Hercules,"[20] comes forth triumphant it will signal the victory of Christ and the triumph of monarchy, the only legitimate and divinely authorized form of government.

Maistre's vision of the conquest of evil forces by religious truth has in its description definite literary overtones. In like manner his support of unwritten law and opposition to man-made constitutions leads him to a comparison of the two in which the contrast is sharpened by juxtaposing political essayists with eminent creative writers: "There is between theoretical politics and constitutional legislation the same difference that exists between poetics and poetry. The illustrious Montesquieu is to Lycurgus, in the general scale of minds, what Batteux is to Homer or Racine."[21]

Much as Joseph de Maistre admired Montesquieu's verve and style he could not abide those features of the *Esprit des lois* which fortified the arguments of constitutionalists. The metaphysical concept of a universal man for whom constitutions were made was vague indeed to Maistre, who never in his life encountered this abstraction referred to so eloquently by republican lawmakers. He agrees with the precept in the *Lettres Persones*, that "one can be Persian"[22] but rejects the hypothetical universal man, a product of fuzzy political thinking.

The crowning paradox for Maistre, who took delight in paradoxes, was the illusion that the people were the dominant force in the French Revolution. Ostensibly it would run counter to common sense and everyday experience to describe a popular movement as the product of one man's machinations. Yet the supposedly democratic character of the upheaval in France was in Maistre's opinion not corroborated by the facts. The masses were not the guiding principle in an historical event essentially totalitarian in nature:

> Not only do the people enter en masse into their great movements solely as the wood and cordages used by a machinist; but even their chiefs are recognized as such only in foreign eyes; and, in fact, they are dominated in the very same way they dominate the people. These men, who, taken together, seem the tyrants of the multitude, are themselves tyrannized by two or three men, who in turn are tyrannized by a single person. . . .[23]

In the 1790s Maistre had in mind the dictatorship of men like Robespierre and Marat. Inadvertently he was describing the situation that would prevail for many years in France under Napoleon. Revolutions in general for Maistre conjured up the specter of unlawful chaos. The revolt led by Cromwell was a notable exception and condoned by basic principles in English law. But while considering the French Revolution totally illicit Maistre could not conceal his amazement at the vigor and violence of the rebellious movement that spread throughout France; he likened it to a miracle:

> The *miracle* is an effect produced by a divine or superhuman cause . . . the French Revolution, and all that is taking place in Europe at this moment, is as marvelous in its way as the instantaneous production of fruit on a tree in the month of January. . . . What is more striking about the French Revolution is this rushing force that suppresses all obstacles. . . . Purity of motives could glorify the obstacle, but that's all. . . .[24]

Assuming, as he does frequently, the viewpoint of a Romantic writer composing an historical novel, Maistre reduces complicated political movements to a simple formula. Just as Maistre perceives in the Revolution primarily an irresistible force, undoubtedly permitted by God to punish man, so he envisages a royalist counterrevolution that would spontaneously sweep France by storm with relatively little advance preparation: "Citizens! behold how counterrevolutions take place. God . . . alerts us never confiding to the multitude the choice of masters. He uses it [the multitude] . . . only as a passive instrument . . . the Roman people took on masters believing they were fighting the aristocracy by following Caesar. That is the picture of all popular insurrections. . . ."[25]

Maistre naively assumes that with the arrival of Louis XVIII in France all opposition will vanish overnight and the army, led by officers eager to ingratiate themselves with the new regime, will unanimously support the restoration of the Bourbons. The Count has little faith in the durability of any republican rule: "How is one to believe in the duration of a liberty that begins with gangrene?"[26] To remove such afflictions extreme means, among them surgery, are frequently required. In the political order bloodshed is often necessary to reestablish peace and tranquility. On a pessimistic note Maistre grimly reminds readers that the current crisis in Europe has no easy solutions: "The terrible shedding of human blood, occasioned by this great upheaval, is a terrible way; but is a way as much as punishment is and it can give rise to interesting reflections."[27]

The need for a counterrevolution in France is evident, Maistre insists, if the French are to realize their manifest destiny as a nation.

All Europe looks to them now for leadership. No country can reject the role assigned to it by the Almighty: "Each nation, like each individual, has received a mission it must fulfill. France exercises over Europe a real authority, that it would be useless to dispute. . . ."[28]

Diametrically opposed to the hegemony enjoyed by France for many centuries in Europe was the pitiful condition of the weak republic established in America. Maistre was irritated by the extravagant claims made for the United States by advocates of democracy in Europe. The Count saw in the new country across the sea a feeble example at best of the potentialities of republican government: "America is cited to us; I know of nothing so aggravating as the praises bestowed on this child in diapers; let him grow up — Not only do I not believe in the stability of the American government, but the particular institutions of English America inspire no confidence in me. . . ."[29]

The monarchistic perspective that pervaded Maistre's thinking is explained to a great extent by his perception of man's subservient relationship to God. All anthropomorphic conceptions of the divinity were repugnant to him. His impatience with bungling attempts to portray divine omnipotence in human terms seems to prefigure Lamartine's frustration with the stubborn refusal of some philosophers to acknowledge God's immateriality.[30] Maistre's close connection with French Romanticism becomes apparent in his insistence on the inadequacy of man-centered explanations of the divine nature: "In a word, man can picture the Creator only by putting himself in relation to Him. Senseless ones that we are, if we want a mirror to reflect the image of the sun, do we turn it towards the earth? . . . For my part I will never believe in the fecundity of nothingness."[31]

The Count was too restless by nature to write a dull political treatise on the state of affairs in Europe. To satisfy his creative instincts he had to express his personal reflections on theology and present a theosophic interpretation of the future of Europe. When he voices his own views on man's relationship to God his affinity to the Romantics at once becomes apparent.

Despite an obvious connection with religion and politics the *Considérations* remains primarily a creative work much like the *Esprit des lois*. With all his erudition Maistre is unable to adhere consistently to a rigorous and disciplined format. The urge to digress and refer to other writers and examples drawn from literature is too strong to resist. With his fondness for paradox and sharp contrast

Maistre converts a Rousseauistic axiom into an outright refutation of the Vicaire Savoyard's pronouncement on the enslavement of the common man. While admiring Montesquieu and adopting some of his principles Maistre relegates the political essayist to a status somewhat beneath that of the poet. Convinced of the supremacy of French language and culture he nevertheless takes examples from both Shakespeare and Homer when wishing to stress a point.

Maistre's view of history is not that of the modern professional historian. He tends to move from particular events to an apocalyptic view of society. Mirabeau, the "king of the marketplace," and Robespierre, the infernal genius of the Revolution, appear more as characters in a drama than stock historical figures. In a sense Maistre prepares the way for the Romantic historians, with their recreation of the past, in works marked by lively and colorful word-portraits. Maistre's style is equally lively and clear although lacking the concrete and exotic terms of later writers. He not only reconstructs the past but conjures up visions of the future. This is a relatively easy task for Maistre since, given his philosophical principles, the future must ultimately bring the restoration of both the Church and the Bourbons.

Underlying the *Considérations* there is a rather frightening symbolism. A satanic force menaces humanity at all times and its most fierce manifestations can be seen in the French Revolution and in similar debacles. The society envisioned by Maistre is not governed by Condorcet's concept of perfectibility or by Leibniz's theodicy that all is for the best. Instead, Maistre perceives a society permeated by evil in a system permitted to exist by a just God who demands atonement for sins committed against His laws. To accomplish this expiation the innocent often must suffer for the wicked. In such an order Rousseau's notion of man's natural goodness is hopelessly utopian. War is an inescapable fact of the human condition and while perhaps the hearts and minds of rulers can eventually be turned to peace it is at best a slow and grueling process.

The poetry of Maistre's pessimistic vision represents the ultimate in grimness. It is all the more forceful in light of its generally accurate insights into human conduct. The basic paradox lies in Maistre's conviction that society will endure in the long run in spite of his bleak picture of France and Europe in the 1790s. With the advent of Napoleon his prophecies in the *Considérations* were unhappily more than amply fulfilled.

II   Fragments sur La France

The *Fragments sur la France* was written in 1793 during Maistre's stay in Lausanne. It was published in the Vitte edition of Maistre's works in 1884 at Lyons.

A Sardinian only by reason of political loyalties Maistre was an incurable chauvinist on the question of the cultural superiority of France. As he does so often in aesthetic and religious matters Maistre relies upon intangible qualities to substantiate his arguments on the quality of French language and civilization: "In order to exercise the kind of supremacy which belongs to it, France has received a forceful language whose hidden character is still a mystery, in spite of all that has been said on this subject."[32]

Maistre's role as a pre-Romantic comes into view here as he expostulates on the mystical virtues of language, a phenomenon beyond the scope of rational analysis. Only a person with a poetic temperament would make such a statement and have the sensitivity to appreciate French writers for the quality of their style. Here Maistre reveals both the Romantic and Classical sides of his thinking. Clarity and *esprit* explain the popularity and influence of the French language: "The good writers of this nation express things better than those of any nation and cause their thoughts to be circulated throughout all Europe."[33]

Although Maistre had pre-Romantic leanings he was not a precursor in the manner of Mme de Staël; he considered the geographic location of the French language a factor that accounted for its beginning. Situated in the heart of western Europe French could exercise a broad cultural influence in either direction, north or south. Mme de Staël would not have accepted this interpretation so clearly in opposition to her own ideas on the merits of Northern literatures. Maistre insisted on the superiority of French letters over other European literatures, even over that of England, whose writers he often treated with respect. English authors, he felt, were fortunate in being recognized, thanks in large measure to their French colleagues who made England known to the literary world: "The throne of this language finding itself placed between the north and the south, it lends itself without difficulty to the organs of other peoples and becomes for them a universal and indispensable interpreter for the exchange of thoughts."[34]

Maistre's cultural chauvinism did not blind him to the merits of foreign writers. In this respect he shared the cosmopolitanism of the *philosophes* and the Romantics who shortly were to appear on the scene. Authors from other countries had their merits, to Maistre's way of thinking. As a diplomat and linguist he could not deny what he had learned by direct experience. But if foreign writers could equal or even surpass their French colleagues in many ways there still remained one point in which France excelled: "It is by the *ensemble* that one impresses."[35] In other words, the literature of the Classical period in France had a unity and oneness in effect unknown to its rivals. Maistre was at heart too much a French Classicist to place the literature of France on the same level with other European literatures.

The very mention of the Classical period recalled to Maistre fond memories of his early reading of Racine and Corneille, writers who in their art revealed a firm devotion to altar and throne. With the eighteenth century, however, Classicism declined and resulted in a "veritable conspiracy against public morals." A sad consequence of this decline was the deleterious effect on French culture: "The arts, which are the expression of the genius of the people, depicted the general corruption."[36] The great and the beautiful were despised in France but English paintings still portrayed noble deeds. Nevertheless, even in England the Regency was plagued by license and debauchery.

Of secondary importance in the *Fragments* are Maistre's political conclusions. As usual his admiration of England and things English is vigorously expressed. Montesquieu would turn pale, Maistre speculates, if he saw the excesses of the French Revolution and might well revise his thinking on the advisability of imitating the English constitution, a step that had only produced bloodshed in France. The constitution drawn up by the revolutionaries and the Encyclopaedia were, in Maistre's estimation, the two most disastrous events of the century. With such a gloomy outlook on political developments in France it is surprising to find Maistre taking a more optimistic view of America. His conclusion is much the same as his interpretation of the revolt in England against Charles I: basic institutions in America remained intact and only the executive was changed. While the federal system had yet to be fully evaluated Maistre had to credit the Americans with far more restraint than their counterparts in France.

The *Fragments* have the advantage of containing Maistre's reflections on French language and literature. His cultural chauvinism is partly justifiable on the basis of the primacy of French letters in the seventeenth century. Among his observations on English literature are remarks that suggest Maistre, if given sufficient time, would have developed into a fair comparatist. He had more than a nodding acquaintance with English, Latin, and Greek writers. Maistre's analysis of French, more intuitional than intellectual, prefigures one of the prominent features of Romanticism. Like many French writers he feels obliged on occasion to play the critic. His negative comments on the Enlightenment are a reflection of his aesthetic and political views. The erroneous politics of the *philosophes* vitiated the quality of their writings and served to increase the alarming spread of corruption whose insidious influence was also seen in the graphic arts. Maistre's acceptance of the American Revolution creates the impression that his political thinking might have changed drastically if he had lived long enough to see subsequent developments in the United States.

III   Essai sur le principe générateur

Alarmed by the French Revolution opponents of its principles countered with their own arguments. This opposition was headed by some of the first representatives of modern conservatism. In England Edmund Burke led the attack with *Reflections on the Revolution in France*, a book that became the bible of many conservatives. On the continent Metternich and Friedrich von Gentz advocated views similar to those of Burke. Among French writers of the same general persuasion were Bonald and Maistre. In *Considérations sur la France* the Count borrowed to a considerable extent from Burke, whom he admired greatly.

The two writers were defending somewhat different traditions. Burke upheld a parliamentary form of government which, despite its imperfections, was by comparison more tolerant than continental absolutism. The English statesman saw the drawbacks of the old French monarchy although he deemed it far preferable to the Terror. Maistre made use of those arguments found in Burke that refuted the theories of the French Revolution; but, in defending the *ancien régime*, Maistre evolved his own theories to uphold the monarchy.

In denouncing revolutionary notions Burke based his reasoning on the tradition of constitutional government in England, as opposed to metaphysical abstractions. Burke explicitly denied that there was any such thing as a right to revolution. No tentative agreement existed between the ruler and the people that could be abrogated by a provocation by either party. Past civil wars in English history were not strictly speaking revolutions, but movements to restore traditional rights that had been usurped.

Maistre followed this reasoning in the *Considérations* by asserting that no people could give itself a constitution. Societies were not created by scraps of paper. The *Essai sur le principe générateur des constitutions politiques* is a résumé of Maistre's views on the relationship of government to Church Church and state. It was written in 1808 - 1809, after the *Considérations* and before *Du Pape* and the *Soirées de Saint-Pétersbourg*. Maistre's forceful expression of opinion in the *Essai sur le principe générateur* earned him the reputation of being a brilliant defender of an objectionable system.

As the intransigent philosopher of absolutism Maistre, through a twist of fate, came into conflict with Louis XVIII, the first Bourbon to regain the throne of France. Maistre had asked Bonald to publish the *Essai sur le principe générateur* anonymously. Unfortunately Bonald misunderstood Maistre's instructions and the essay was printed in 1814 under the author's name, and appeared just after Louis XVIII brought out a charter modeled on the constitutional monarchy of England. By this strange coincidence the loyal supporter of the Bourbons appeared in an adversary relationship with the *ancien régime* in the early days of the Restoration.

Implicit in Maistre's opening statement in the *Principe générateur* is the blithe assumption that his point has already been proven to the reader's satisfaction. With this assurance Maistre broaches the question with his customary incisiveness: "One of the great errors of the century that professed them all, was to believe that a political constitution could be written and created *a priori*, whereas reason and experience unite in establishing that a constitution is a divine work, and that what is precisely most fundamental and most essentially constitutional in the laws of a nation could not be written."[37]

Here the rhetorical technique of Rousseau is applied in reverse and perhaps with superior skill and unction. The Age of Enlightenment was the period of widespread error, the reader is told, and no explanation is necessary, therefore, to justify the conclusion drawn at the very outset. Maistre informs readers that the remainder of the text will merely enlarge on what is already an incontrovertible fact.

After ridiculing Locke's notion of the role of the collective will of the group in forming the character of laws Maistre refers nonchalantly to "primordial good sense" that takes precedence over "sophisms" in tracing the origin of basic laws to the divine will.[38]

The author's early legal training manifests itself in a statement that a clever attorney would make before the court: "The real *English constitution* is this public spirit, admirable, unique, infallible, above all praise." In view of this fact a written law becomes secondary and ephemeral in importance and even ludicrous: "One cannot conceive how a sensible man could dream of the possibility of such a chimera."[39]

Throughout the essay Maistre is equally concerned with the effectiveness of his style and the exposition of his ideas. Sentences of relatively moderate length and capable of being quoted separately as maxims are interspersed through the text. In the matter of a justifiable *coup d'état* Maistre states the solution succinctly: "Man cannot create a sovereign. At best he can serve as an instrument to dispossess one sovereign and hand his estates over to another sovereign already a prince."[40]

He never tires of presenting the *philosophes* in a bad light. "The eighteenth century which suspected nothing, doubted nothing" that supported its pet ideas. "The greatest folly, perhaps, of the century of follies, was to believe that fundamental laws could be written *a priori.*"[41]

Not satisfied with a repetitive strain of irony Maistre, out to titillate his readers, employs a *reductio ad absurdum* to drive home his point. If Plato was right in declaring that man did not learn through the written word alone, then there must be a higher form of knowledge transmitted directly to man. This being the case the advocates of written constitutions are indeed to be pitied: "Now, I say it without the least spirit of contention, and without claiming to shock anyone, they show by that as much philosophy and true learning, as though they were looking for the real dimensions of man in an infant in diapers. . . . "[42]

On the subject of American Indians Maistre takes the outspoken Condorcet to task for empty promises. What proposal could be more preposterous than that of Condorcet who suggested the *philosophes* could be of great assistance to the Indians! Whereas most white men abused them Catholic missionaries alone had Indian interests at heart. The Paraguay Reductions under the auspices of the Jesuits demonstrated all too clearly the depth of the Church's commitment to uplift the aborigines. By contrast Rousseau's nonsense about the need to imitate the Indian was sheer drivel from a mad man who did not speak from firsthand experience.

Voltaire was equally to blame in making statements not based on actual observations. The crafty *philosophe* spoke on everything "without ever having pierced a surface." If Voltaire is serious in claiming that the selling of judgeships is an example of one abuse spawn by another, then the reader is obliged to conclude that Voltaire "had only on rare occasions the time to think." An abuse is an evil or deficiency, not an existing institution, asserts Maistre, who in a more serious tone stresses the need for established and honored legal traditions. Happily Voltaire never had charge of the courts, otherwise they would have fallen into the hands of adventurers and have been snatched from families devoted to law. After picturing vividly the dire consequences of a mismanaged legal system Maistre, mindful of his own family's role in the magistrature of Savoy, solemnly ends the discussion: "The more it is penetrated by the divine principle, the more durable it will be."[43]

In employing all the tricks of rhetoric and satire to please the reading public Maistre appears as the *littérateur*. He is too inclined to relax after having made a point to be the relentlessly logical philosopher.

No self-respecting metaphysician would breathe a sigh of despair in the midst of a syllogistic *tour de force* to complain about the continuing influence of the eighteenth century: "Alas! it has ended only in our almanacks."[44]

It would be a distortion to portray Maistre as a magnanimous and sympathetic writer always willing to concede the good points of his adversaries, but he was not totally incapable of doing so. On occasion he was rather objective and dispassionate. Attracted by the clarity and quality of Bayle's style Maistre admires the power of Bayle's logic when "he fought materialism in the article LEUCIPPE of his dictionary." Having only a passing acquaintance at best with some of Bayle's major writings Maistre shrewdly sensed "the father of modern incredulity" did not resemble "his successors." Unlike them he was often "more fair to the good cause than to the bad."[45] Maistre had no way of knowing that Bayle was probably a precursor of modern, liberal Protestantism with his own version of the leap toward faith. The incisive attacks by Bayle on superstition are now considered by many scholars to be merely his method of purifying the mind prior to entering into a closer mystical relationship with Christ. As far as it went Maistre's analysis, in light of present research, is fairly accurate.

The *Essai sur le principe générateur* is a handy compendium of Maistre's basic concepts in the field of philosophy and political science. As is so often the case his wit and irony embellished by a clear, concise style give the work a certain literary polish. His antagonistic attitude toward the eighteenth century constituted the *mal du siècle* which plagued him during his career and which was the motivating force in the composition of his best works. This antagonism produced something more than the rantings of an embittered polemicist for the royalist establishment. It was in a sense the final chapter of the Enlightenment and served to add a much needed dimension to the literary masterpieces of the *philosophes*, for the picture was not complete without the writings of a distinguished Catholic author who profited by his reading of Voltaire, Rousseau, and Montesquieu.

IV   Étude sur la souveraineté

The *Étude sur la souveraineté* was written in Lausanne during the period 1794 - 1796. It remained unpublished until it appeared first in the Vitte edition of the complete works.

"The people are sovereign, it is said; and over whom? — Over themselves apparently."[46] Thus begins the *Étude sur la souveraineté*, with Maistre stressing at the outset the ridiculous paradox in his mind of a multitude possessing the centralized authority of a monarch. The people have nothing to say in the matter, he sternly warns. God created society and provided it with necessary laws. All theists, believers in some form of divine revelation, agree that the worst type of law-breaking was to deliberately oppose the divine ordinances.

"It is a strange mania of man's to create difficulties for himself in order to have the pleasure of solving them."[47] Maistre cites this axiom to explain to his own satisfaction the plethora of erroneous theories during the Enlightenment on human origins, man's function in the world, and the government best suited to man's needs. All reasoning of this nature is superfluous, especially since everywhere it is evident that human beings were designed to live together in social groups.

Any deviation from the normal social pattern is patently an exception to the rule. It is futile to resort to isolated examples of nomads wandering about in the desert cut off from the civilized world. Equally absurd is any effort to theorize about man's state prior to the organization of society. Before man became a social being his state of development was too incomplete to warrant any serious speculation on the significance of humanity's most early beginnings. For this reason it is entirely illogical to attempt to make a clear cut distinction between the state of nature and the social state when the latter represents the natural condition common to most men on earth: "The word *nature* is one of these terms which one abuses like all abstract terms. This word, in its widest acceptance really signifies only the sum total of all laws, all forces, all jurisdictions that *make up* the universe. . . ."[48]

In no way could the term nature be used to describe or define the wild imaginings of a Rousseau concerning the alleged origins of mankind. One egregious example of Rousseau's careless thinking was the so-called original contract between the people and the person chosen as ruler. Since society in the Maistrean sense evolves from the natural order of things established by God, Rousseau's vague notion of a contract is of no earthly use to anyone interested in the truth concerning human evolution.

Edmund Burke sums it up aptly for Maistre when he says, "Art is the nature of man."[49] The real man of nature is the person who has all the knowledge, arts, and affections usually associated with human activity. By that token the weaver's cloth is as much a part of nature as the spider's web. Nor does the American Indian, Rousseau's favorite model of pure primitivism, furnish a sound argument for thinking otherwise. If anything, the Indian represents a fallen state, a deviation from the universal order of things. Even in his savage way of living the Indian still is a member of a society governed by a ruler.

Much as Maistre probably felt the urge to continue the assault on Rousseau's pet theories he had more important goals in the *Étude sur la souveraineté*, among them the evil of the French Revolution. When such a catastrophe sweeps the country ordinarily little resistance is expected. If substantial resistance does occur it is nothing short of a miracle. To Maistre the counterrevolution in the Vendée was a remarkable demonstration of loyalty to altar and throne: "The other malcontents of the kingdom, although in much greater number, could not effect anything equal [to it] because these malcontents are only *men*, whereas the Vendée is a *nation*."[50]

The action of the Vendeans was that of a people defending time-honored institutions. An examination of the sacred books of ancient civilizations discloses the solemn religious significance attributed to the coronation of monarchs and the privileges bestowed on them by heaven. These truths come from the cradle of humanity in the Near East regardless of the furious denials of the *philosophes*. In one of his numerous blunders Rousseau attempts to rule out the divine right of kings, a privilege he reserves for a hypothetical legislator in some distant period of history. But how, Maistre asks, can this notion offer anything uniquely new and startling when Rousseau admits that the legislator is gifted with divine insights? "Everything is good in his works, except his systems."[51]

Focussing his attention on ancient languages to reinforce his thesis of the presence of the divine plan in the universe since the dawn of time, Maistre speaks of the antiquity of Eastern languages, Hebrew, in particular, being in all probability the most ancient. To support this statement he cites the research of Sir William Jones (1746 - 1794), the British orientalist who popularized the study and knowledge of Asiatic languages and cultures. Among the early legislators of the Near East Maistre mentions Moses, one of the greatest lawgivers and for all practical purposes king of his people.

Even Rousseau was obliged to express his admiration for Judaic law in one of many implicit refutations of his own theories. The Hebrew code was incontrovertibly a direct gift from God. Other religions were not totally devoid of a superior revelation. Mohammed, in the Koran, provided a religious basis for government and for legitimate authority.

When referring to models of the type of government he championed Maistre speaks warmly of English institutions and the Magna Carta as an example of divinely inspired unwritten law. By designating England as a smoothly functioning monarchy Maistre endeavored to rebut the *philosophes,* to whom Great Britain was one of the best proofs of the success of constitutional government. For similar reasons he goes to great lengths in the *Étude sur la souveraineté* to negate the conception of Rome as one of the first great republics. The customary arguments in favor of a republic were all nonsensical anyway. Insignificant entities like Switzerland and the Italian city states had little to offer in the first place. Most laughable of all was the attempt to portray Rome as a republic. Rousseau's oracular pronouncements to the contrary, the Romans in the main always acknowledged some sort of central authority.

Mention of Rousseau inevitably obliged Maistre to give equal time to Voltaire. The witty rationalist is raked over the coals for encouraging revolt against legitimate political and religious powers. Together with Rousseau Voltaire is accused of causing the French Revolution. Maistre did not judge Voltaire totally reprehensible and applauded the latter's definition of the Athenian democracy as the government of the *canaille.*

Nostalgia invoked by the memory of the splendors of the reign of Louis XIV haunts Maistre as he harks back to the glories of France's illustrious past when *belles lettres* flourished. The patronage of Louis XIV supported many outstanding writers and artists of the Classical period. In fact, reigning monarchs frequently inspired great works of literature. A case in point was the composition of epic poems in honor of various kings from the *Aeneid* of Virgil to the *Henriade* of Voltaire.

In the *Étude sur la souveraineté* Maistre was not always guided by a partisan spirit. His praise of the Koran implied hidden admiration for the accomplishments of the Arabs when they ruled Spain and North Africa. Readily conceding that Christian Europe was relatively benighted in the period of Arab hegemony, Maistre lauds unequivocally Moslem contributions to the arts and sciences.

Another non-Christian era also becomes the object of Maistre's praise when he traces the essential character of European governments to the Teutonic tribes: "It is in the midst of the forests and ice of the North that our governments were born. It is there that the European character was born. . . . "[52]

Although Maistre believed in the cultural superiority of France the allusion here to the Northern countries of Europe recalls the prominence given to the culture of the North by Montesquieu and Mme de Staël. As such it is additional evidence of Maistre's pre-Romantic tendencies and ideas. In the same vein is a description, employing a favorite Romantic symbol, of the change wrought in the person speaking in God's name: "A drop of this immeasurable Ocean of existence seems to stand out and fall upon the man who speaks and acts in the name of divinity."[53] To many Romantics the ocean was a symbol of infinity, and Maistre's use of it singles him out as a writer who by temperament had much in common with the authors of Romanticism.

The *Étude sur la souveraineté*, while primarily a treatise on political science, discloses a good deal concerning Maistre's literary inclinations, for the basic themes are common among writers of the Enlightenment and the coming generation of Romantics. His conceptions of the true primitive man and of the beginnings of society and culture were to be shared by subsequent writers unimpressed by Rousseau's version of the noble savage. Mérimée and others were to view the individual in a relatively barbaric milieu as an impulsive and straightforward type devoid of the deceit of more sophisticated people but definitely not blessed with a streak of natural goodness. Isolated tribes might appeal to the imagination but were at best oddities separated from the mainstream of nations.

Similarly, nature was not used by Maistre in any naive sense to denote simple natives close to the soil. Instead, nature signified to him the finest accomplishments of civilization, its laws, arts, and sciences. This, he contended, was the real meaning of a term that Rousseau had abused too often. Maistre's negative reaction to Rousseau on the implications of the word nature links him with Realists and Naturalists who revolted against the worn-out Rousseauism of the Romantics.

When Maistre referred to things ancient he went back to earlier stages of man's history, when civilized institutions began to flourish. His speculations about Hebrew as the oldest language and his allusions to Asiatic languages and to sacred books other than the Bible show him to be ahead of his time. The Romantics were fascinated with the disclosures about man's origins in Asia. The revelations of the Hebrews along with those of the Moslems and Hindus struck their imagination, for in these sources of human culture they beheld a pristine poetry. Nothing enthralled the Romantics more than the panorama of world religions, a sign of God's continuing revelation. What is surprising is that Maistre abandons his customarily inflexible position as an orthodox Catholic to entertain the possibility that other religions possessed their share of theological truth.

Maistre has much to say on politics in the *Étude sur la souveraineté*, but when praising the merits of monarchy he also notices the extent to which epic poems flourished under kings. The most splendid period to him is the reign of Louis XIV. With all his devotion to Classicism, Maistre seems to accept here a principle of relativity. Since Maistre recognizes with Montesquieu that governments vary according to customs and needs, he probably assumes the same relativistic perspective in judging literary movements. Classicism has had its day, he may well have concluded, so therefore literary expression in the future will take a different course. Such an assumption would explain his preoccupation with Romantic themes like the Northern tribes, ancient languages and religions, and the concept of primitive man. The political theorist evidently had too active an imagination to restrict himself wholly to dry academic considerations.

CHAPTER 3

Du Pape *and Related Works*

I   *Background and Publication of* Du Pape

DURING his residence in Saint-Petersburg Maistre became friendly with Monseigneur Severoli, Archbishop of Ragusa and Vatican nuncio at Vienna. This friendship raised Maistre's hopes of obtaining strong support for his work on papal authority, *Du Pape*, already in progress. The Count wrote to Monseigneur Severoli in 1815 expressing great confidence in the ultimate success of *Du Pape*, "I would even believe myself in a position to make a society of atheists understand that they have on this point the same interest as we do."[1]

Maistre's detractors seize upon this statement as a sign that the Count at bottom was a cynical atheist who, for some strange reason, thought adherence to a conservative Catholic position would somehow further his own designs on achieving personal glory and power. Nothing could be further from the truth. The passage in question represents a technique frequently used by the crafty polemicist in conjecturing his probable success among those strongly opposed to his views. If theoretically he could convince them, he is saying, then success is automatically assured.

When Maistre received news that his ambassadorship in Russia was terminated he wrote Severoli again about his plans to meet the prelate in Rome. Approval of *Du Pape* by the Vatican was uppermost in Maistre's mind as he planned a publicity campaign for his forthcoming book. Unfortunately the Count, after his return to Chambéry, could not make the projected visit to Rome.

Unable to obtain the desired patronage from Rome Maistre turned next to Chateaubriand. The distinguished author of the *Génie du Christianisme* complimented the Count on the excellence of his work but at the same time respectfully declined the offer to edit *Du Pape* and assist in its publication.

41

Disappointed but undaunted, Maistre called upon a highly respected scholar, Abbé Vicarin of Geneva, for advice about publishing *Du Pape*. The priest, while a firm believer in papal authority, was nonetheless disturbed by the audacity of the work's contents and referred *Du Pape* to other scholars in the hope that by scrupulous editing they could soften the tone. Maistre calmly accepted all corrections and *Du Pape* was finally published at Lyons by Rusand in December, 1819. No amount of editing succeeded in mollifying hostile readers, who took offense at the Maistrean barbs directed at the non-Catholic forces in Europe. Lamennais and other church leaders in France praised *Du Pape* enthusiastically. At Rome comment was restrained; many looked askance on Maistre for his extremist views and wondered how an upstart layman expected to add anything new to doctrines on papal authority.

With its defense of the papacy's role in European affairs *Du Pape* forms a theological corollary to Maistre's political treatises. Papal infallibility is the first subject treated since, after having established this fact, the author can proceed to deal rather easily with other facets of the question. In insisting on the infallibility of the pope and the Catholic Church Maistre points to the role played by Catholicism for eighteen centuries as historical justification for his assertion.

One of the first items on Maistre's agenda is the subject of Church councils, especially those in the early period after the death of Christ. These councils were the point of departure for many subsequent disagreements on doctrine. The orthodox Churches in the East and the Church of England maintain that the councils definitively established that only all bishops acting together could decide doctrinal matters. The pope as bishop of Rome was just another prelate and not a divinely appointed chairman dominating the councils. Maistre enjoys assailing the Anglicans and the Orthodox Christians for what he considers their presumptuousness. To the doughty polemicist tracing papal authority to Christ's designation of Peter as head of the Church was a simple matter requiring little exposition.

In keeping with a time-honored tradition among Catholic apologists Maistre quotes at length the testimony of the Church Fathers to support his position. Patristic texts and usages are examined to shed light on the nature of the early Church. Leo III's pontificate is seized upon as a useful example by Maistre to demonstrate that by the fifth century Leo III was already acting in essentially the same manner as modern occupants of the throne of Saint Peter. No stone is left unturned by Maistre to muster all available evidence in support of the Supreme Pontiff. The records of the Anglican and Orthodox Churches are investigated to produce evidence that at one time they accepted the pope unequivocally as head of Christendom. Within France, Maistre points out, this was true of the Jansenists and Gallicans. Bossuet, caught in the midst of the Gallican controversy, defended, at least to Maistre's satisfaction, the primacy of the Vatican.

From the premise of papal infallibility Maistre, as a political philosopher, draws positive conclusions in the hope that a stable order based on divine law will be restored to Europe. The history of Europe provides Maistre with numerous examples both of the power exerted by the pope over recalcitrant rulers and of the wars waged directly or indirectly by the Holy See against Moslems, heretics, schismatics, Protestants, and kings who defied papal sovereignty. What Maistre recommends is a peaceful status quo in Europe made possible by the submission of heads of state to the Vatican. If this were done, political and religious strife would be kept at a minimum.

With peace and order assured, Maistre is confident the Catholic Church could easily carry out its mission to preach the gospel. Slavery in foreign lands would be abolished and the dignity of woman's status would be honored. Unlike Protestant missionaries of the Bible Society, which Maistre vigorously disliked, Catholic priests would prevail through their superior calling and the spiritual strength derived from the practice of celibacy. To accomplish the divine objectives of the Church continued cooperation from the priests and nuns and from kings sanctioned by God was of the utmost importance.

Du Pape ends with a plea to the Orthodox Churches to return to the fold. Acceptance of the Orthodox branches by Rome would be relatively uncomplicated, since they had kept the apostolic succession of bishops and the sacraments. Conversion of Protestants and *philosophes* would be difficult but not impossible. Having weathered the Reformation and the French Revolution the Catholic Church was equal to the task.

In the preface to the second edition of *Du Pape*, written on July 1, 1820, at Chambéry, Maistre answers opponents of his work who accused him of not following Church teaching, by stating "the dogmas and even the maxims of lofty Catholic discipline are in great part only divinized *laws of the world*" and that "the words *sovereignty* and *infallibility* are two natural synonyms."[2] By establishing an argument based on reason Maistre sought to bolster the proofs of papal authority derived from Catholic doctrine and from the interpretation of Scripture.

Du Pape also represented an effort on Maistre's part to prepare Christians for the two phases they had to undergo in the readjustment demanded by the divine plan after the bloodbath of the Revolution and the Napoleonic Wars. Expiation and regeneration were expected of Europe in Maistre's view. "Our order during the last century has been extremely guilty vis-à-vis religion . . . the Church is beginning again . . . it will still be able to astonish us by its knowledge." This reasoning was closely tied to another recurring theme in Maistre's work: "We are touching on the greatest of religious epochs."[3] The Count felt that France was a key nation in the general return to the fold of the Catholic Church that he anticipated. This widespread movement was necessary to counteract the effects of the French Revolution: "It is *satanic* in its essence. It will never be totally extinguished except by the opposite principle." The antidote to Jacobinism was of course religion, which, properly speaking, was the Church headed by the pope; to accomplish the total extinction of revolutionary heresy Rome had to be accorded due recognition by the kings of Europe: "We ask only that it enjoy the right common to all possible sovereignties which all act necessarily as infallible."[4]

After declaring his position on the pope's authority and infallibility Maistre proceeds to take aim at his favorite targets, the *philosophes*. Hume is treated summarily, like a refractory schoolboy, for daring to criticize the Council of Trent: "If one omits from this passage the insult and tone of scurrility . . . there remains something true, the more the world is enlightened the less one will think of a general council."[5] Associating universal gatherings of the Church with the Middle Ages Maistre fails to see their relevance to modern times, an assumption disproved by recent developments in the present century

Voltaire is the recipient of several tongue lashings in *Du Pape*. Invariably Maistre quotes passages from Voltaire's histories to show how the caustic *philosophe*, by careless and ambiguous statements, supports more often than he denies the theory of infallibility. Rousseau as well is ridiculed by Maistre for vacuous and unfounded remarks on clerical celibacy.

The Count's interest in literature asserts itself throughout *Du*

Pape. Linguistic analysis especially attracts Maistre, who speculates on the close relationship between the spoken language and the symbols developed to record that language in writing. He also discerns intangible elements in this relationship: "The mysterious correspondence between languages and the signs of the writing is such, that if a spoken language is pedestrian, the writing will be pedestrian too; if the spoken language is vague and awkward and has a difficult syntax, then the written form will also be wanting in elegance and clarity."[6]

Maistre's sensitivity and reaction to language and style are, as stated elsewhere, that of a Classicist. Among the greatest achievements of French literature for him were the works of the seventeenth century. Pascal and Bossuet were quoted frequently in *Du Pape*, as much for their style as for their thinking on the pope's prerogatives. Maistre cites the Jansenist writer more often than Bossuet in support of infallibility. The latter's equivocation on Gallicanism irritates Maistre to the point where he cries out, "What spiders' webs! What subtleties unworthy of Bossuet!"[7]

With all his admiration of the French language and the writings of the Classicists Maistre would logically seem a member of the Moderns in their continuing quarrel with the Ancients in the dispute that began in the seventeenth and lasted through the eighteenth century. His training in Latin under the Jesuits however produced the opposite result. In *Du Pape* he insists on the universality and superiority of Latin and regrets the disappearance of Latin inscriptions from statues and coins, one of the incidents that precipitated the quarrel of the Ancients and Moderns!

Let anyone cast his eyes on a map of the world, let him trace the line where *this universal language* became silent; there are the borders of European civilization and fraternity. . . . The French . . . forgot this language almost entirely; they have forgotten themselves to the point of causing it to disappear from their coins. . . .[8]

While *Du Pape* reveals Maistre's Classical side there is ample evidence as well of a Romantic temperament in his idealization of the Middle Ages. With almost nostalgic longing Maistre conjures up visions of past glory when popes summoned armored knights to join the Crusades against the Moslems in the Holy Land: "As for just wars, holy and necessary in themselves, such as the Crusades, if the popes *provoked* and sustained them with all their power they did well and we owe them an eternal thanksgiving. . . ."[9] This defense of a justified militarism in certain religious wars encouraged by the Vatican does not harmonize with another passage in *Du Pape*, in which Maistre berates the military tone of the English constitution as a menace to freedom: "A certain soldierly spirit, which is the gangrene of liberty, threatens rather clearly the English constitution; I willingly ignore other symptoms. . . ."[10]

Continuing in this peaceful vein Maistre takes delight in reminding readers that the Catholic ideal of an orderly acceptance of any legitimate authority is far preferable to Protestantism, which foments rebellion and scoffs at the Catholic policy of peaceful acquiescence: "Protestantism, on the contrary, taking as a point of departure the sovereignty of the people, a dogma which it has transported from religion to politics, sees, in the system of *non-resistance*, only the final debasement of man."[11]

Maistre's adherence to a modified form of pacifism suggests that inwardly he detested war, although he saw no remedy for bloodshed on the battlefield to accomplish certain goals. What other method could remove Napoleon and restore the Bourbons? When speaking of freedom, of course, Maistre meant that man was free to enjoy the benefits of lawful authority ordained by God. In rejecting Rousseau's precept of man's natural goodness Maistre recalls that human nature was vitiated by the Fall and thus unable to exercise properly the prerogatives of complete freedom: "Aristotle even went . . . so far as to say *that there were men who were born slaves*. . . . The one who has sufficiently studied this sad nature knows that *man in general*, if he is reduced to himself, *is too wicked to be free*."[12]

The theory of natural slavery propounded by Aristotle is applied specifically to women. As usual Maistre's remarks do not ingratiate him with exponents of liberation. In the Count's estimation women owe much to Christianity for being placed on a pedestal. This recognition is accorded women who fulfill a servile function in a convent or in the home. Maistre's notion of the adjusted female has no room for an egocentric Mme de Staël: "Woman more than man is indebted to Christianity. From it she derives all her dignity. Christian woman is truly a *supernatural* being because she is uplifted and sustained by it in a state which is not *natural* for her. But with what immense services does she pay for this kind of ennoblement!"[13] Such remarks on the feminine role in society in Maistre's correspondence leave little doubt that he assigned the fair sex to a subordinate place in society. They had to be content, he felt, with supernatural rewards. Less condescending and more enlightening were the Count's observations on Russia in light of that nation's hegemony in Europe in the twentieth century: "A beautiful phenomenon is that of Russia. Placed between Europe and Asia, it derives from both. The Asiatic element it possesses and which meets the eye should not humiliate it. Rather one might see in it a claim to superiority. . . ."[14] *Du Pape* is not merely limited to considerations of the Vatican's role in Europe but embraces other facets of European history and social organization.

II   *The Message of* Du Pape

Much of the underlying message of *Du Pape* is a none too subtle recollection of the good old days, *le bon vieux temps,* of a unified Christendom under the pope in medieval times. For Maistre the new order he foresees will combine the best features of the Middle Ages and modern Catholic thinking. By implication *Du Pape* is Maistre's artistic manifesto as well, for art in the purest sense can only thrive in a cultural milieu regulated by religious truth. In several ways *Du Pape* is a conservative Catholic answer to the more liberally oriented *Génie du Christianisme;* the book by Maistre has a eulogy of the clergy toiling in missionary fields and of the role of priests in society much like Chateaubriand's praise of the Church's- work. Whereas the *Génie du Christianisme* appeals to man's sensibilities by stressing the sensuous beauty of Catholic liturgy and practice, *Du Pape* calls upon leaders and scholars in the Church to help reestablish Catholicism by recognizing the rightful authority of the pope.

As the orthodox equivalent of the *Génie du Christianisme* Maistre's work took its place as the conservative explanation to the young Romantic movement of the meaning of Catholicism. *Du Pape* is also the one work which identified Maistre as a politico-religious thinker and it assured him a place among the leading philosophers of absolutist thought in the Metternich era. The book's cogent style and clear exposition of Maistre's premises made it popular in Catholic and politically conservative circles. Thanks to *Du Pape,* Maistre became the symbol of the old order and reactionary theology to both liberals and *littérateurs.* Opposition to his ideas did not hamper the ability of opponents to admire his wit and clarity. Maistre's fondness for Bossuet and dislike of the Jansenists, while it did not endear him to Romantic writers, was still substantial proof of his literary interests. Sainte-Beuve and others deplored Maistre's reactionary tendencies although entertaining considerable esteem for the aesthetic merits of his style. *Du Pape* has literary value as an expository piece of writing and assures Maistre a place among other figures like Tocqueville and Guizot, remembered for their style as well as for their contributions to French political and religious thought in the nineteenth century.

III   De l'Église gallicane

De l'Église gallicane dans son rapport avec le Saint-Siège was originally intended by Maistre to form part of *Du Pape;* subsequently he changed his mind and made it a separate work. The subject, Maistre freely admits, was highly controversial since Frenchmen had fixed opinions on the issue of Church relations in France with the Vatican. Maistre's purpose was to address himself to future problems that conceivably might arise, and predictably he saw a return to legitimately established authority as the only plausible solution. The French clergy had to take the only logical course, submission to the Holy See, not merely in faith and morals but also in jurisdictional matters, including the thorny question of appointment of bishops by Rome rather than by the French government.

De l'Église gallicane was in the process of being prepared for publication over a long period of time and finally appeared in the second edition of *Du Pape* in 1821, just before Maistre's death.

Maistre objects to the term Gallican, which implies a branch of the Catholic Church with certain inalienable rights of its own. If allowed to go unchallenged, the concept of a Gallican Church would be accepted in the same sense as that of the Anglican Church. With this statement as a point of departure Maistre considers Calvinism and Jansenism, their relations with secular governments, and their status as religious movements opposed to papal authority. Calvinism resulted in political and religious chaos. Its offspring, Jansenism, preached a doctrine that had much in common with Hobbes. Both the English philosopher and Jansenius implicitly denied man any freedom of choice by making the principle of necessity take precedence over any apparent exercise of free will. On the question of the influence of Port-Royal on education and literature Maistre scoffs at their unearned reputation and dismisses them as pesky troublemakers. For Pascal Maistre has much esteem but expresses regret that so lofty a mind became infected by Jansenism.

The controversy that raged between Louis XIV and Pope Innocent XII on whether the papacy or the monarchy had the right to appoint bishops and govern the internal affairs of the Catholic Church in

France was a difficult subject for Maistre to handle. An objective evaluation was hard to make, since the Count admired spokesmen of both sides. Innocent XII had Maistre's support, but the usually outspoken polemicist was reluctant to criticize harshly the actions of Louis XIV, whose reign and accomplishments he respected, and Bossuet, to his mind one of the great orators and writers of Catholicism.

Louis XIV, though an exponent of Gallicanism, often acted correctly, Maistre is moved to concede, in light of the Revocation of the Edict of Nantes and the disciplinary action taken against the Jansenists. In the case of Bossuet's position on the Gallican issue, Maistre is loathe to assign Bossuet arbitrarily to the Gallican camp in view of the archbishop's overall loyalty to the pope. Instead, he prefers to see Bossuet as a cautious moderate more intent on healing wounds than causing ruptures. When forced to declare his stand on the Gallican question, Bossuet sincerely favored the king's jurisdiction in the French Church over the pope's, without compromising his integrity as far as Maistre is concerned.

In the first part of *De l'Église gallicane* Maistre alludes to the confusion and disunion in Calvinism and Lutheranism and at the end of his works perceives the same defects in Gallicanism, which was established by parliamentary license and not by legitimate ecclesiastical authority. Even Voltaire was right in concluding that the Gallicans, by speaking of liberties, implied they were free to some extent from Rome. No such liberties exist in fact, Maistre asserts; on the contrary, Gallicanism is a threat to the unity of France. Only the good will of the Holy See has prevented a more serious rupture.

In *De l'Église gallicane* Maistre rails against Jansenism and Port-Royal, which were to remain favorite topics among nineteenth-century critics and historians. Maistre's antagonism toward the Jansenists sums up the conservative, Catholic stand on the issue. Never was his invective more biting than in his assaults on Port-Royal:

Some melancholic sectaries, embittered by the prosecution of the state, had the idea of locking themselves up in a solitary spot in order to sulk and work there at their ease. . . . Pride, resentment, religious rancor, all the bitter and hateful passions are unchained at the same time. The concentrated partisan spirit is transformed into incurable rage. . . .[15]

As a literary historian Maistre has fair powers of discernment. He appreciates the contributions of Pascal and the literary merits of the

Lettres Provinciales, a "very pretty libel,"[16] that left its mark on the French language. Arnauld, Nicole, and Tillemont were persons of distinction, and, though the remaining writers were definitely second-raters, Port-Royal, despite its threat to throne and altar, served as a rallying point for *prosateurs* in an era when poetry was the chief preoccupation of *littérateurs.* The *Pensées,* another menace to Christendom which was almost "hanged"[17] by this book, rates high in Maistre's estimation. Pascal ranks with Bossuet as an eminently sincere man capable of discerning the sincerity of others; the assessment of Descartes by Pascal is considered very just and accurate. Aside from the accomplishments of Pascal and a few other well-known writers Maistre assigns the greater part of the Port-Royal fraternity to oblivion: *"The rest are not worth the honor of being named,* most of these names are even profoundly forgotten."[18]

The indisputable shortcomings of the Jansenists were unwittingly described, to Maistre's amusement, by a would-be apologist: "The elegant pen of Mme de Sévigné confirms perfectly . . . while believing to render a panegyric, the atrocity of Jansenist dogmas, the hypocrisy of the sect and the subtlety of its maneuvers. This sect . . . is still the most vile because of the falseness that characterizes it. . . ."[19] Mme de Sévigné was only one of a number of distinguished writers who, Maistre claims, were exploited by Port-Royal to enhance its own public image. Jansenists took advantage of the normal anticlericalism found in any Catholic country to publicize its own cause at the expense of the Church. Never did any group divide and conquer as insidiously as the Jansenists of Port-Royal described by Maistre: "Port Royal took over the time and talents of a rather large number of writers who could make themselves useful . . . divided the Church . . . embittered minds and got them used to resisting; it fomented suspicion and antipathy. . . ."[20]

What was ludicrous about Port-Royal's devious attempts at self-aggrandizement was the dearth of talent in its own ranks. According to Maistre the center of Jansenism in France had little to brag about: "Not only was the talent mediocre at *Port-Royal* but the circle of this talent was extremely restricted, not only in sciences properly speaking but in knowledge which is most definitely related to their position. . . ."[21]

However, if the limited intellectual resources at Port-Royal forced the Jansenists to rely on outside support, notably that of Pascal, they did have the advantage of promoting the use of French in their propaganda, which thereby addressed itself to a wider reading public. As students of the Classical languages they were barely adequate: "But nothing increased the power of Port-Royal over public opinion more than the exclusive use they made of the French language in their writings. They knew Greek without doubt; they knew Latin, but without being hellenists or latinists, which is very different . . . they could not even compose Pascal's epitaph in good Latin. . . ."[22]

Maistre seizes upon Port-Royal's alleged inferiority in Latin scholarship to refute the contention of La Harpe that the Jansenists were better Latin teachers than the Jesuits:

La Harpe surprises me very much when, in some section or other of his Lycée, he decides *that the recluses of Port-Royal were very superior to the Jesuits in the composition of elementary books.* I do not inquire whether the Jesuits were created to compose grammars . . . except when this small superiority would be worth the trouble of being disputed. . . .[23]

After listing any number of textbooks in Latin produced by Jesuits Maistre washes his hands of the affair, in order to consider more serious matters. There is much in favor of the Count's contention that the Jesuits played an important role in seventeenth-century France. The Society of Jesus had many capable members who wrote works on literary criticism and philosophy that exercised a substantial influence on French literary circles. In adhering to this line of reasoning Maistre also insists that Pascal learned nothing from Port-Royal. Instead, the Jansenists were endebted to him for his formidable pen, which he used so effectively in their defense: "Pascal spent four or five years of his life in the walls of Port-Royal where he became the center of attraction without owing it anything; but without wishing in any way to detract from his real merit which is very great, one must also confess that he has been overly praised. . . ."[24]

Faced with the necessity of minimizing the prestige of Port-Royal even at the risk of criticizing Pascal, one of his favorite models of a Christian writer, Maistre is obliged to disparage the Pascal who defended Jansenism. A similar choice confronts Maistre on the question of Bossuet's antipapal position in the Gallican controversy. The Count does his best to depict Bossuet following a neutral course in the dispute between Louis XIV and the Vatican: "Bossuet entered into the assembly as a moderator. . . . He did not want anyone to treat the authority of the pope; this frightful imprudence must have

shocked a man whose most striking quality was the fear of compromising himself with any authority. . . ."[25] As with Pascal Maistre
displays an obvious impatience with Bossuet's failure to support the
pope more firmly but refrains from bitter criticism of a Catholic
writer he nonetheless admires.

The main emphasis of *De l'Église gallicane* is on the theological
aspects of the Gallican controversy, a subject still meaningful to
French readers. The same problems raised by Louis XIV's assertion
of authority were repeated in the confrontation of Napoleon with the
Vatican. Jansenism was of course a subject that arose fairly often in
nineteenth-century French literature. From a literary standpoint *De
l'Église gallicane* throws more light on Maistre's views on literature
than *Du Pape*. His digressions on Pascal, Bossuet, Port-Royal, and
Jansenism were noted by subsequent writers and critics like Sainte-
Beuve. In the nineteenth century no single writer was perhaps at
once so cordially esteemed and disliked as Maistre. Readers were
both fascinated by a clear scintillating style, reminiscent of the
philosophes, and repelled by a school of thought that stressed the
worst features of a hard-line on a Catholic and royalist establishment. A few writers of the nineteenth century approved of this phase
of Maistre's thinking; others reacted violently against it. To many
Romantics Maistre's name became synonymous with the *ancien
régime*. Understandably, during the Restoration of the 1820s his
philosophy affected writers at a moment when Catholicism and
Bourbonism were in vogue. Later, the literary world as a whole
turned against Maistre, the arch-Catholic reactionary, but maintained its respect for Maistre, the stylist.

IV   Lettres sur l'Inquisition espagnole

Maistre begins the *Lettres sur l'Inquisition espagnole* with an
historical survey of the Church's campaigns against heresy; he
focuses his attention on an early theological revolt against
Catholicism that eventually turned into a civil conflict. The Albigensians who flourished in southern France in the twelfth and
thirteenth centuries preached that the body represented the evil
power and the spirit the good principle in man. Extremists among
the Albigensians advocated suicide as the only escape from a wicked
world. The religious and civil authorities, led by Saint Dominic,
crushed the Albigensians by armed force. Maistre hastens to point
out that the Church represented the sole moderating influence in
any open attack on heresy. This was particularly true, he maintains,

of the Spanish Inquisition, where the administration of physical punishment came under the civil arm. Because of the more clement disposition of the ecclesiastical court the Templars, when arraigned for trial, wanted the clergy to sit in judgment.

Maistre is expecially indignant at Montesquieu's criticism of the Spanish Inquisition in the *Esprit des lois*. The Spaniards did not burn Jews at the stake, he insists, because of their religious and cultural origins. To do so would have been unthinkable: "An innocent young girl, burned in the great capital of Europe, with no other crime than that of believing in her religion would be a national crime so horrible it would suffice to stigmatize a population and perhaps an entire century. . . ."[26]

Much of the talk about the Inquisition in Spain and Portugal Maistre finds inaccurate. If atrocities in human torture and imprisonment did occur they were not as outrageous as Queen Elizabeth's persecution of Puritans, Rebels, and Catholics. At least in defense of Spain, Maistre protests, it can be stated that by the Inquisition the Spanish were trying to maintain a high degree of spiritual purity. France, he implies, would do well to imitate the strict Catholicism of Spain.

Maistre's reading of Montesquieu leads him to take issue with the latter on the subject of the Spanish Inquisition. Reacting favorably to the artistry of Montesquieu but unfavorably to his deistic slant on religious practices in Spain Maistre, with his customary vigor, objects to an attack on the Spanish Inquisition, one of the prime targets of the writers of the Enlightenment in their campaign against intolerance. Moments such as this earned Maistre the reputation of a bitter and benighted fanatic, although such was not the case. In his own judicial career in Sardinia Maistre usually acted mercifully and equitably, and he makes it clear in the *Lettres sur l'Inquisition espagnole* that he opposes anti-Semitism. As for his defense of the Church's role in the *auto-da-fé*, Maistre is on the whole correct in blaming the brutality on the civil officials instead of the ecclesiastical court. Anxious to correct historical inaccuracies Maistre is inclined to go to the other extreme and to whitewash the Catholic Church's involvement in the suppression of heresy. From this standpoint Maistre is no better or no worse than many *philosophes,* who verbally assaulted Catholicism with little regard for an objective evaluation of the facts and through a desire to present rationalism in the most favorable light. With the bloodshed of the French Revolution fresh in his mind Maistre considers past offenses against humanity by Church and State relatively minor.

CHAPTER 4

Soirées de Saint-Pétersbourg

THE *Soirées de Saint-Pétersbourg ou Entretiens sur le gouverne-ment temporel de la Providence,* written during the long years spent by Maistre in Saint Petersburg, remained unpublished until after his death. In the *Soirées,* a series of *entretiens* or conversations, there are three participants, the Count — none other than Maistre himself — a Russian Senator and a young French aristocrat, living in exile in Russia.

Available evidence indicates that the Russian Senator was a certain Tamara, former ambassador from Russia at the Turkish court in Constantinople and brother-in-law of Kotochoubei, a well-known minister of the Czar. An enthusiastic disciple of German mysticism and Swedenborg he appears in the *Soirées* as a defender of theosophy and the peculiar mixture of science and mysticism so popular in eighteenth century Germany.

The third figure of the *Soirées,* the Chevalier, seems to be an amalgam of three persons taken from actual life. One source identifies the French nobleman as the Marquis de Romance-Mesmon, a close friend of Maistre, but he was too old to be the impetuous young gentleman of the *Soirées.* Another researcher names the Comte de Blacas as the model of the Chevalier. The best evidence, however, points to the Chevalier de Bray as the one who corresponds most closely to the émigré of the *Soirées.* In 1809, the date assigned by Maistre to the *entretiens,* the Chevalier de Bray was the Bavarian ambassador at the Russian court. Bray appears to be the primary source for Maistre's impulsive émigré, who has an intimate knowledge of the German intellectual world.[1] Still, there is sufficient reason for believing that Maistre incorporated as well in his Chevalier certain facets of the personalities and viewpoints of the Marquis de Romance-Mesmon and the Comte de Blacas.

I *First* Entretien

On a hot July evening in St. Petersburg in 1809 the Count takes his two companions, a Russian Senator and a French Chevalier, to his summer home in the country. The trip is made by boat. On their arrival the three friends relax and the young émigré speculates on the manifestation of God's justice in the world. Immediately the Count strikes up what proves to be a lengthy conversation; the Senator quickly predicts a series of discourses lasting indefinitely in the manner of Scheherazade's story-telling in the *Thousand and One Nights*. The main theme is stated by the Count, in reply to the Chevalier, as the consistency of God's justice in regard to both mankind in general and the individual in particular. If God is the creator of all things, then it seems to follow He is the author of evil. This notion is discussed at some length, with the Count insisting that evil is an absence of good and not a separate existing entity. Examples are quoted from the Hindu religion and Catholicism on the nature of virtue and vice. At this juncture the Count and his friends feel the need to adjourn until the following evening.

II *Second* Entretien

After finishing their tea the Count, Senator, and Chevalier continue to explore the question of the existence of evil. In the course of their discussion they touch on original sin, Platonism, the origin of man, comparative religion, religious practices in India and China, the Greek concept of a Golden Age, the divine origin of language, and the limitations of human reason. The Count in his analysis of the foregoing points assails the *philosophes* and quotes Thomas Aquinas in support of his own position. On an optimistic note the Count ends the conversation with a happy prediction that the unity of mankind is not far off.

III *Third* Entretien

Are all forms of sickness merely the consequence of crime or sin? The Senator poses this question as a starting point for the third *entretien*. The Count responds by reminding the Senator that God's laws are immutable and that accidental occurrences in the universe do not alter their course. Degradation and chaos seen in the world result from man's fall, not from divine will. Excited by the Count's arguments the Senator adds several observations in support. Now the Chevalier takes a more active part in the conversation by remarking that vice always appears to triumph over virtue. When the Count seeks to disprove such an assumption the Chevalier capitulates and looks forward to another session.

IV *Fourth* Entretien

Prayer is very much on the Chevalier's mind and he requests the Count to discuss it in some detail. Glad to oblige, the host outlines the omnipotence of God and the manifestations of His power in the universe. Annoyed when the Chevalier quotes Voltaire, the Count excoriates the sage of Ferney for undermining the values derived from prayer and religion. The Senator joins in and cites Saint-Martin on the necessity of prayer. Abruptly the subject changes to physical evils inflicted on man as a punishment. Voltaire's poem on the disastrous earthquake at Lisbon is recalled, although the Count rejects categorically Voltaire's pessimism and endeavors to minimize the importance of seemingly frightful catastrophes in light of God's ultimate mercy and justice. The late hour and the increased activity of mosquitoes oblige the Count and his guests to retire.

V *Fifth* Entretien

Casual remarks by the Senator concerning a fireworks display on the previous evening, interspersed with complaints about mosquitoes, serve as a preface to the fifth meeting. When the Senator theorizes on the range and limit of animal knowledge the Count is unable to resist the urge to distinguish sharply between the process of cognition on the sensory and intellectual levels. There follows a lively exchange of opinion between the Count and Senator on the nature of causality and the properties of physical substances. Progress in the sciences during the seventeenth century is praised by the Count, who maintains that even the sixteenth century had good scientists despite Bacon's criticism of the scientific shortcomings of his own century. Before they take leave of one another the Senator expresses interest in examining in the near future the Chevalier's inquiry about war and its place in the divine plan.

VI *Sixth* Entretien

Eager to continue the discussion on the benefits of prayer the Count explains how Fénelon recommends that the average man should admit to God the extent to which worldly distractions interfere with any effort to pray. When the Senator suggests that Locke has useful advice on equating desires with their object the Count dismisses Locke as inconsequential and returns to Fénelon and the need to base prayer on faith in order to pray more effectively.

Somewhat mischievously the Chevalier demands an explanation for the Count's dislike of Locke and receives in reply a stinging denunciation of the English philosophers' sensism and its errors in misinterpreting the operations of the human mind. Locke fails to understand how man forms a concept or a mental picture of the essence of external objects. By contrast Newton, the Count explains, does not refute the principle of immateriality that prevails in Creation and has a correct conception of divine causality. The *Essay Concerning Human Understanding* becomes the object of the Count's wrath owing to Locke's denial that man has innate ideas. Worst of all is the deleterious influence of Locke on the *philosophes*. Exhausted, the Count suggests that the Chevalier question the Senator the next time. All agree that the lively exchange of ideas was typical of a conversation among Frenchmen given the nature of their language.

VII *Seventh* Entretien

Determined not to be put off any further, the Chevalier insists that the Senator speak out on the subject of war. Pleased at the Chevalier's insistence, the Senator sketches the roles of the soldier and the executioner; the former is praised for the nobility of his tasks while the latter is despised for the brutality of his. While the Senator expounds in some detail on the problems of a just war, the motivations of the soldiers, and the present impossibility of world peace, the Chevalier and the Count take turns raising difficulties. The Count steers the conversation into another topic, the Bible and the Psalms, and with the Senator contemplates the beauties of the Scriptures. Night and its symbolism in the Bible also come under their scrutiny. The Chevalier interrupts them to announce he is retiring.

VIII *Eighth* Entretien

The three friends discuss the Chevalier's proposal to publish their discussions. Although skeptical of the success of such a venture, the Count agrees with the Chevalier to consider the *entretien* as the basic form of their chats owing to its intrinsic orderliness, as opposed to the digressiveness of the conversation and the artificiality of the dialogue. In recalling topics discussed at their previous meetings the Count reviews his notions on prayer, suffering, and original sin. In order to comprehend these matters the existence of God must be acknowledged. The fact of His existence is established by the order

of the universe despite the attempted refutations of the *philosophes*.
The Senator interrupts the Count's tirade to inform him and the
Chevalier that it is too chilly to remain on the terrace.

IX *Ninth* Entretien

No time is lost in picking up the threads of the previous night's
debate as the Senator gives the floor to the Count. Without hesita-
tion the latter tells how the most evident truths often seem con-
tradicted by experience. For example, hereditary monarchy is established by divine ordinance, but facile arguments win over many
to a specious democracy. In times of chaos and revolution the innocent must frequently atone for the guilty. In the midst of
enumerating examples of this type of atonement in the historyof
Christianity the Count all of a sudden digresses to entertain the
possibility that Seneca became a Christian. The lateness of the hour
induces the Count to call it a day and to retire with his guests.

X *Tenth* Entretien

The Senator and the Chevalier strike up a conversation on the
meaning and function of sacrifices. Commenting on the tendency of
man to form family and social units the Senator notes how one person may suffer hardships for the entire group; he enters again into
the larger question of the laws of Providence. The presence of unseen laws and mysteries is alluded to by the Senator who gives a
rather theosophic view of the workings of the universe. Agreeing
with the Senator wholeheartedly the Count tries to demonstrate that
there is no intrinsic conflict between Christianity and theosophy on
the one hand and true science on the other, provided that the
erroneous conclusions of the *philosophes* are disregarded. The
Chevalier fears that the Count tends to associate theological truths
too closely with scientific facts. Despite the Count's denial the
Chevalier continues to downgrade science and advances the
possibility that so-called superstitions in reality represent certain
preternatural revelations known to the common people through the
ages. Quite willing to admit the truth of this last statement the
Count adds that the supreme indulgence, the Redemption, by which
individuals were ransomed from sin, illustrates the type of truth in-
accessible to scientific analysis. One of the central themes of the *entretiens*, the principle of reversibility, namely that the innocent must
suffer for the guilty, provides the note on which the Count ends the
discussion.

XI *Eleventh* Entretien

Merrily teasing the Count about his reluctance to converse on frivolous topics the Chevalier demands to know why the spiritual order should not be subjected to scientific scrutiny. The Count retorts that certain truths are better left unexamined to prevent extravagant speculations of the type propounded by misguided German illuminists. A Frenchman, Louis-Claude de Saint-Martin, was also an illuminist who sincerely inquired into universal arcana hidden from man, observes the Senator; the Apocalypse of Saint John, certain portions of Scripture, and revelations other than those contained in the Bible clearly demonstrate that an incalculable store of mysteries remains concealed from man. Delighted by the Senator's defense of Saint-Martin, the Count eulogizes the French illuminist who touched on basic religious truths in his writings — unlike the vagaries of his counterparts in Germany. Although not wishing to start a lengthy discourse on the arcana revealed by Saint-Martin and other theosophists with valid insights into sacred verities, the Count expresses his willingness to entertain the prospect of a new epoch of wondrous revelation in the not too distant future. At this point the text abruptly ends.

In an *Esquisse du morceau final* the Count affectionately bids farewell to the Chevalier and tells him to fight bravely on the field of battle, where he might well fall an innocent victim in atonement for the current sins of society. To the Senator the Count gives lengthy advice on avoiding petty plots at the Russian Court by becoming a Roman in spirit and cultivating the arts. Poetry would be a proper escape valve for the Senator in the trying period ahead. The Count assures the Senator he will always cherish fond memories of Russia.

XII *The* Soirées *as a Creative Work*

Maistre has in mind a definite format for the *Soirées* and allows the Chevalier to detail precisely the advantages of the procedure followed in their discussions:

Let us not confuse terms: *conversation, dialogue* and *entretien* are not synonyms. The *conversation* rambles by its very nature. . . . But the *entretien* is more suitable . . . the *entretien* is subject to the rules of dramatic art which do not admit a fourth speaker. . . . As for the *dialogue,* this word only represents a fiction; for it supposes a conversation that never existed. . . .[2]

It is apparent that Maistre regards the *Soirées* primarily as a creative work. Three participants in the *entretiens* lend a Classical balance to the drama that unfolds. There is no room in Maistre's scheme for a fourth person with another point of view. The Sardinian ambassador at Moscow, having suffered enough from the French Revolution and Napoleon, only has time to concentrate on those opinions that are more or less in agreement with his. If an opposing view is given it is merely for the sake of argument, with the Count refuting all hostile opinions at will. The drama that takes place is Maistre's picture of three men discussing the destiny of Europe and Christianity on the eve of what will hopefully be a new order, with the restoration of legitimate religious and political institutions.

Some sensitivity to the physical beauty of nature is displayed in the opening pages where Maistre depicts the brilliance of the setting sun as the group travels on the Neva River toward the Count's summer home: "Its disk surrounded by a reddish haze rolls like a fiery chariot over the somber forests which crown the horizon, and its rays reflected by the windows of the palaces, give the spectator the impression of a vast conflagration. . . ."[3] With an appreciation of the plastic aspects of nature rather typical of the early Romantics Maistre combines metaphors already used by neo-Classical poets with a few concrete descriptive terms. His view of nature here foreshadows that of Lamartine; a serene setting constitutes the point of departure for a serious meditation on the philosophical implications of existence. Maistre, however, does not have the patience to sit and brood. From the eighteenth century he has acquired a taste for controversy. Only a brief pastoral interlude precedes the main order of business, the consideration of what God holds in store for mankind.

Surrounded by the bloody horrors of war and revolution that promise to continue indefinitely, the three friends often take a grim view of society. Regrettably, war seems to be ethically normative for man, sadly remarks the Senator, and even in peace violence is also a part of everyday life. Two professions, that of the soldier and of the executioner, become symbols of a social order which must live with violence: "The soldier and the executioner occupy in effect the two extremities of the social scale. . . . There is nothing so noble as the first, nothing so abject as the second. . . ."[4] The executioner emerges as a majestic, if somewhat macabre, figure in Maistre's perception of the social order, for the very preservation of society depends on the horrible function of the *bourreau*, in the Count's analysis. Without *him* mankind is doomed to disorder and turmoil: "Take away this in-comprehensible agent; in an instant even order gives way to chaos. . . . There is then in the temporal circle a divine and visible law for the punishment of crime; and this law . . . has been executed in-variably since the origin of things. . . ."[5]

Maistre goes on to illustrate how war ennobles man if fought in a just cause, although when waged to accomplish evil it debases nations. Elsewhere, through the various speakers, Maistre admits a dislike for war; but since it is an inevitable part of the human condi-tion he feels it must fit somehow into the divine plan. In like manner the suffering of the innocent to atone for the sins of the guilty, which Maistre calls the theory of reversibility, represents another equally mysterious but necessary phase of divine justice: from the beginning of man's history the concept of sacrifice has been an important part of human institutions.[6]

Inclined to be consistent with the premises he has stipulated, Maistre has the Count explain why in view of the evil in the world the necessity of war and the suffering of the innocent are quite un-derstandable. Original sin especially sheds considerable light on the reasons behind human imperfection: *"Physical evil could enter into the universe only by the fault of free creatures; it can be there only as a remedy or expiation, and consequently it cannot have God as a direct author. . . ."*[7]

Clearly a God known for his justice had to provide some recourse for sinful man obliged to spend a certain period of years in this vale of tears. So-called rationalists had tried to destroy even this consola-tion God intended for mankind: "The philosophy of the last century . . . overlooked nothing in order to distract us from prayer through the consideration of *immutable and eternal laws.*"[8] In their discus-sion of the salutary effects of prayer the Senator and the Count con-sider the treatment of this subject in the Bible and in pagan writers. The Senator explains how prayer traditionally is less efficacious after sunset: "Light intimidates vice; night gives it back all its strength, and it is virtue that is afraid."[9]

The Count for once assumes a more cheerful outlook and sees no essential conflict between prayer and night time. Has not the Church sanctified the dark hours through its ritual and liturgy? What the *philosophes* attempted to steal from Christians, namely faith in prayer, has been retained thanks to its supernatural character and the beauty of Catholic practices. Prayer in the evening hours always remains a source of strength to the Christian: "It is the period of profound meditations and sublime ecstasy; in order to profit by these divine impulses. . . . Christianity for its part has taken hold of the night, and consecrated it to holy ceremonies which it animates by austere music and powerful canticles. . . ."[10]

Maistre's insistence on the struggle of the human spirit in his time to overcome the insidious effects of deism is one of the recurrent themes in the *Soirées*. Locke's system of explaining everything by material causes alone shocks Maistre's sensibilities. Surely, the Count insists, the aesthetic qualities of life were not conceivable without an element of the mysterious and spiritual. Through his theory of the origin of ideas Locke would deprive mankind of any basis for believing in the beautiful: "There is not, I believe, anything more debasing or dreadful for the human spirit. Through him reason has lost its wings and drags itself along like a slimy reptile; through him the divine source of poetry and eloquence was silenced. . . ."[11]

To Maistre, Locke, who hoped readers would not regret their purchase of the *Essay Concerning Human Understanding*, represented the basest sort of materialistic thinking. "What a stench of the marketplace!"[12] the author of the *Soirées* exclaims in expressing his disgust with Locke's commercialism and callous disregard for man's higher faculties and potentialities. By way of overthrowing any rationalistic hypothesis on the supremacy of human reason Maistre traces the origin of language to God: "No language could be invented, neither by a man who would not have been able to have himself obeyed, nor by several men who would not have been able to understand each other. . . . *It sprang forth before the beginning of time from the bosom of its principle; it is as ancient as eternity. . . . Who can relate its origin?* . . ."[13]

Owing to the divine origin of language many truths were revealed directly to man through the terminology necessary to understand them. God literally inserted the required words into the mind of man. For that reason the oldest civilizations, which existed closer to the time when human beings were first created by God, had a fresher and clearer concept of truths revealed to them supernaturally: "The sages of antiquity although deprived of the knowledge we possess, were however closer to the origin of things, and some remains of the primitive traditions had come down to them. . . ."[14]

Closely allied to such concepts as the divine origin of language and God's direct revelations to man at the dawn of civilization were the teachings of the "elegant theosophist,"[15] Louis-Claude de Saint-

Martin, with whom Maistre became acquainted during his association with Masonry. A mystical quality perceived by Maistre in Martinism attracted him to theosophy, an ideology in direct opposition
to the incisive polemicist's customary dogmatism. The *Soirées* bear
witness to the continued influence of Saint-Martin on Maistre, who
felt that the theosophist bolstered Catholic teaching by the revelation of preternatural verities not in conflict with Church doctrine. It
is therefore not surprising to find the Count expounding the Martinist notion of an ethical instinct in man: "It is one of my favorite
ideas that the upright man is rather commonly warned, by an inner
feeling of the falsehood or truth of certain propositions before any
analysis, often even without having made the necessary studies to examine them. . . ."[16]

A preference for the irrational and intuitional marks a *volte-face* in
the *Soirées* for Maistre, speaking through the Count. Other ideas
stemming from Martinism and expressed in the *entretiens* are the existence of an invisible order of things parallel to that in the visible
world and the importance of prayer in the religious life of the "man
of desire,"[17] Saint-Martin's term for the disciple initiated into the
mysteries of theosophy. Maistre became an exponent of Martinism
early in his career. What appears an odd step for an orthodox
Catholic was an understandable reaction on the part of many
believers to the rationalism of the *philosophes* at the time. Saint-
Martin seemed an eloquent spokesman for spiritual values in an era
of irreligion. The depth of Maistre's hostility to attacks on
Christianity is made clear to readers in the scathing criticism of
Voltaire by the Count. Voltaire's familiar rictus and biting remarks
on Christian beliefs are subjected to Maistre's caustic analysis.

At · least the Count in the *Soirées* is fair in treating other
philosophes with equal scorn. Rousseau does not escape criticism; his
doctrine of the natural goodness of primitive man is ruthlessly examined. Maistre refuses to admit that the virtuous but uncivilized
primitive man ever really existed. Instead, he insists that the savage
represents a period of decline in a given culture, which in its primordial state enjoyed a certain degree of civilization. In Maistre's view,
prior to the Fall man received directly through the divine gift of
language considerable knowledge of the arts and sciences. Arguments of this type, with their stress on human reliance on God,
counteracted the rationalists' emphasis on the reasoning powers of
the individual. As with Voltaire, Maistre castigated other *philosophes* like Diderot and Condillac. Although Rousseau tended to

favor the intuitional in man Maistre still considered him an opponent of supernatural values and grouped the Vicaire Savoyard with
the rest of the *philosophes*.

When it is a question of style and artistry the *philosophes* fare
somewhat better in the *Soirées*. The Count readily acknowledges the
literary powers of Rousseau and Voltaire, although he prefers the
more Christian orientation of French writers of the seventeenth century. Maistre's aesthetics remain essentially Classical. To the Count,
Corneille's *Polyeucte* is morally superior to the *Barbier de Séville;*
the level of aesthetic perfection in a work of art is established by its
clarity and unity of composition.

Much as Maistre revered the past he kept pace with current
developments. The Count discourses glibly on the findings of the
Hindu scholar, Sir William Jones, and suggests that Chinese civilization may antedate the culture of India. Since there was then considerable discussion in England and Germany on the literary aspects
of the Bible, the Count praises the psalms, attributed to David, and
the stirring passages of Genesis ascribed to Moses. Interest in the Bible and the ancient civilizations of Asia were to become preoc-
cupations of the Romantics. In this regard it is interesting to note
that the Count's description of his own method of composing a
literary work is surprisingly non-Classical, Maistre's stated preferences to the contrary: "Often I put down as well those thoughts of
the moment; those sudden *illuminations* which are extinguished
without bearing fruit if the inspiration is not recorded in writing. . . . Each passage awakens in me myriads of interesting ideas
and melancholy souvenirs. . . ."[18]

Maistre is aware of pre-Romantic forces already at work and
recognizes that certain English writers have been publicized in the
rest of Europe through French versions of their writings: "Young,
Richardson, etc. have been known and enjoyed in Europe only
through French translations and recommendations."[19] These
authors of course played a significant part in the spread of literary
ideas and techniques that contributed to the development of
Romanticism on the Continent.

Assessing the function of the poet throughout history, Maistre
perceives Horace as more than a master of form and structure: "He
knows how to *spread* the divine voice about the human ear like a
sonorous atmosphere which still resounds after God has ceased to
speak."[20] The association of the poet with the creation of beautiful
sound effects in the exercise of a priestly function has a distinctly

Romantic quality. Such a tendency becomes more apparent in Maistre's appraisal of David the psalmist's view of nature: "If he descends to particular phenomena, what an abundance of images! What richness of expression! Behold with what vigor and what grace he expresses the *nuptials* of the earth and the moisture. . . ."[21]

The power of the artistic imagination fascinates Maistre and in commenting on Raphael he marvels at the painter's ability to create a world of fantasy despite the fact that the Italian master's most imaginative paintings still have a definite link with the real world: "The inexhaustible imagination of Raphael could cover his famous gallery with fantastic combinations, but each work exists in nature."[22]

Maistre's essentially Romantic impulse reveals itself as well in his views on the relationship of poetry and prayer. He accepted the axiom of Saint-Martin that "Prayer is the respiration of the soul" and believed that "Every legitimate prayer" arises "like a beneficent dew which prepares us for another homeland." Through prayer, Maistre implies, a higher form of poetry is achieved; the psalms of David bear witness to this: "Man despite his degradation always wears visible traces of his divine origin," a Pascalian affirmation of humanity's lofty station in the universe. The privilege enjoyed by man is fortified by his ability to speak directly to God: "Prayer is the *dynamic* confided to man."[23]

At this point in his theology when speaking of prayer Maistre abandoned the cold reason of logic employed in polemics in order to become an advocate of irrationalism, that is, of a belief which relied on intuition and faith to explain a universe regulated by mysterious powers. Poetry lends itself readily to such a system of belief highly Romantic in its implications. Mysteries remain to be discovered in the world and the poet is the logical one to head the exploration.

Saint-Martin held sway over Maistre's thinking; the theosophy of the "unknown philosopher" encouraged an irrational *Weltanschauung* and satisfied the Count's curiosity about spiritual phenomena not countenanced by rationalists. Like the French Romantics of the nineteenth century Maistre, a child of the Enlightenment, required additional teachings to bolster the doctrines of the Church. Prayer, poetically defined by Saint-Martin, was more than a sterile series of mindlessly repetitive litanies. When the "elegant theosophist" spurned those who sought to debunk religion his rebuttal had the freshness of a typical comment. "*Let the imprudent chemist run the risk of adoring his own work*"[24] was a typical observation with a contemporary flavor aptly designed to poke fun at the follies of rationalism.

Rejection of the ludicrous claims of scientists constituted a main part of a religious outlook deeply impregnated with irrationalism. The Count, adhering firmly to his position, left no stone unturned to counter the arguments of the *philosophes.* If they ridiculed popular beliefs, presumably unverified by science, then Maistre had little compunction in defending any allegedly unreasoning fear of the unknown. The Chevalier's remarks in this regard are strongly supported by the Count: "Superstition then is neither *error* nor *fanaticism.* . . . It must be then something *beyond* legitimate belief. In truth, there is nothing to get excited about. . . . In love, in friendship, in fidelity . . . superstition is likable, precious even and often necessary; why would it not be the same with piety? . . ."[25]

Elsewhere Maistre refers slyly to "agents of a higher order" to show that he places no limits on the invisible world. Closely connected with Maistre's irrationalism is the concept of time. "Temporal order," he suggests, "is . . . the image of a higher order."[26] It is a state where the restrictions of earthly existence no longer obtain and time as a measure of change ceases to exist. The past, present, and future intermingle to present a perspective of all events placed on one level. Memory, stirred by an external object, creates this almost Proustean sensation in Maistre: "Each passage awakens in me a swarm of interesting ideas and melancholy souvenirs a thousand times sweeter than all that people commonly call *pleasures.*"[27]

The Count's obsession with the limits imposed by time led him to place great value on the role of prophecy in men's lives. Saint John in the Apocalypse transcended the barriers of time to make prophecies that Maistre felt applicable to the aftermath of the French Revolution. A new era, he felt certain, had to be established by God to counteract the pernicious effects of Jacobinism. Maistre makes it clear, in describing the function of David in the Bible, that the prophet and the poet are one and the same in the theosophic sense he gives to the terms. Materialists unfortunately remain blind to prophecy and its poetic message. For this reason Maistre does not pause in a relentless campaign against the *philosophes.*

Maistre has great hopes for the future and foresees "The prophet enjoying the privilege of leaving time behind, his ideas being spread no more in a measured existence."[28] The Count's conception here of the poet-prophet's mission is rather sophisticated by modern terms and implicitly grants the poet considerable licence in the use of themes and imagery. There is no mistaking what Maistre has in mind. No adroit selection of quotations is required to illustrate a point that the Count asserts firmly and clearly. He seeks an answer to the great enigma of the unseen world about him and an explanation to the irrational forces at work in man. The facts are all too evident to shake Maistre's belief in the validity of irrationalism:

The prophetic spirit is natural to man and will not stop asserting itself in the world. Man, trying in all periods and in all places, to penetrate into the future, declares that he is not made for time; for time is *something forced which only asks to be ended.* Whence it comes that in our dreams, we never have the idea of time and that the state of sleep was always judged favorable to divine communications. . . .[29]

For Maistre the irrational order is undeniably a part of the divine plan and is mentioned in the Bible. Saint-Martin assumes the office of mystical exegete in clarifying baffling passages of Scripture containing instructions to the faithful which only the theosophist through preternatural insights can recognize and interpret. Among the hidden truths deciphered are the existence of a primitive revelation, the invention of language, the forecast of an epoch of expiation to be followed by an era of regeneration. In terms of everyday living, man learns that reality has another dimension yet to be realized. While not referring specifically to the subconscious Maistre definitely envisages this very aspect of the psyche both in depicting man's desire to defy time and in outlining the still unexplored realms of the dream world.

Not discouraged by the prevalent skepticism of his own period, an unwelcome legacy of the Enlightenment, Maistre confidently predicts a genius will appear in the future who will reconcile the two orders, rational and irrational:

That one will be famous and put an end to the eighteenth century which still lingers; for intellectual centuries do not regulate themselves by the calendar as do *centuries* in the proper sense. Then opinions, that today seem to us either bizarre or unreasonable, will be axioms which no one will be permitted to doubt and people will speak of our present *stupidity* as we speak of the superstition of the middle ages.[30]

Illuminists of the Martinist school will be the leaders in receiving and publicizing the exciting revelations in the millenium confidently predicted by Maistre. The Golden Age will herald the union of all religions, among them Christianity, Judaism, and Islam. The Count differs with the usual line of reasoning among illuminists concerning a nonsectarian cult and prophesies instead a union of all creeds under Rome. Except for this divergence from the standard theosophic position Maistre adheres to the basic principles of Martinism.

The Romantic side of Maistre asserts itself when he is not engaged in metaphysical arguments. With the *philosophes* out of the picture his thoughts dwell on less controversial issues. The persistent recurrence of observations on literature and style despite the amount of time spent in argument and refutation reveal all too clearly Maistre's longing to address himself more to literary and aesthetic questions. That he was caught between conflicting tendencies as a creative writer is apparent from his work. While in style and vocabulary he was part of the Classical tradition of the seventeenth and eighteenth centuries he was in many respects already an instinctive Romantic. Nowhere is this more evident than in the Senator's prediction that in a not too distant period man would be provided with both a new revelation and increased knowledge: "And do not say that all is said, all is revealed and that it is not permitted to us to expect anything new . . . in the matter of divine knowledge there is much lacking to us, and as for future manifestations, I have, as you see, a thousand reasons to expect them. . . ."[31]

The Romantic vision of a millenium stated above was a commonplace in utopian poetry and social philosophy in the first half of the nineteenth century in France. By joining the ranks of those who anticipated a modern version of the Golden Age Maistre, although that was not his intention, momentarily left the camp of orthodox Catholicism. Believers in a millenium espoused many beliefs not sanctioned by the Church, a second physical coming of Christ, direct revelation of hidden arcana to the initiated, and other occultist concepts unacceptable to Rome.

XIII   *The Historical Significance of the* Soirées

With all its contrasting themes and tendencies the *Soirées de Saint-Pétersbourg* constitutes a provocative document of the period of transition between the Enlightenment and Romanticism. Three representatives of the old social order sum up the present state of things and speculate on the future of Europe in 1809. The time is well chosen, for Napoleon will remain in power only six years longer. War has been a fact of life for the Count, the Senator, and the Chevalier, hence it is one of the major problems they confront. The inevitability of bloodshed is symbolized by the significance attributed to the roles of the soldier and the executioner or *bourreau*. The latter is Maistre's symbol of the penalty God exacts from society in payment for man's sins. Long established traditions show the need for sacrifice in the order of divine justice. If the innocent must often atone for the guilty, then this principle is entirely in accord with the consequences of original sin. Maistre becomes another Saint John in presenting a metaphorical and apocalyptic view of society emerging from the godlessness of the Enlightenment, the French Revolution, and the tyranny of Napoleon.

The indictment of the *philosophes* for their pernicious effect on civilization presents no difficulties to Maistre, who scorns them for undermining throne and altar, the very foundations of a sound society. In an effort to relegate Voltaire and the *philosophes* to oblivion Maistre unleashes the full force of his invective. A moderating factor is provided by those sections of the *Soirées* that depict the solace supplied by the Christian concept of prayer. Even in the gloom of night the individual soul can meditate on things divine. Immediate communion with God is facilitated by following Catholic practices and the teachings of Saint-Martin, which reinforce the doctrines of the Church.

Maistre's aversion to rationalism and his espousal of Christianity are intimately connected with his aesthetic views. The Enlightenment posed a threat to man's spiritual values, the source of true poetic inspiration. Christianity's contributions to world literature could be seen in the scriptural writings of Moses and David and in the Christian writers of seventeenth-century France. From his religious frame of reference Maistre derives two aesthetic principles at first glance seemingly in conflict. One principle insists on a Classical purity and unity in any work of art and the other allows for a Romantic concept of spontaneous inspiration quite apart from any logical planning in the composition of the work at hand. The combination of these two principles can be seen in the *Soirées* where Maistre, in the clear and rigorous prose of Classicism, considers ideas to be given full expression later by writers of French Romanticism.

In a sense Maistre, like Chateaubriand, stresses the importance of the Christian factor in literature. Both agree on the function of prayer and the aesthetic quality of Catholic liturgy, but there the similarity ends. There is no room in Maistre's literary symbolism for the Christianized Rousseauism of Chateaubriand. Original sin replaces natural goodness as the prime motivation of human conduct. Prayer does not remove man from the harsh realities of every-day experience and the terror of night with its attendant evils. Dreams of a utopian order are counterbalanced by the grim reminder that war, in the foreseeable future, will still exact its toll. There is a definitely satanic undertone to Maistre's perception of contemporary society. If the *Génie du Christianisme* contains a message of sweetness and light for a public weary of an arid rationalism, the *Soirées de Saint-Pétersbourg* reminds Europeans that no Christian vision of the human condition is complete without the admission of the persistent effects of original sin and the resultant dichotomy in man's nature.

The most clairvoyant phase of Maistre's thinking in the *Soirées* is contained in his pronouncements on the poet-prophet in relation to man's endless frustration with the strictures imposed upon humanity by time. Maistre indicates to the poets of the future the unlimited possibilities they have to defy time through the eternal talent and capacity of the true artist to create an art form in which the illusion of time no longer exists. In the subconscious world, Maistre predicts, man will realize more fully his potential and the powers at his command as the most gifted creature in the scale of God's Creation.

XIV *Joseph de Maistre and Saint-Martin*

The extent of Saint-Martin's influence on Maistre through *L'Homme de désir* is generally acknowledged although never studied primarily as a literary source for the *Soirées*. From all reports Saint-Martin was a very pleasant individual and Maistre, though inclined to be critical in his comments on other people, was charmed by the elegant and gentle theosophist who visited him at Chambéry in 1787. Although this is their only recorded contact it is quite probable they had met previously when Maistre went to Lyons to be initiated into the arcana of Masonry. Saint-Martin eventually broke relations with the Masons owing to dissatisfaction with the rationalism rampant in many lodges. The theosophist, nicknamed the "unknown philosopher," preferred to induct *candidats* individually into his own circle.[32] In his writings Saint-Martin publicized the tenets of his particular brand of illuminism and, although he never formally organized his followers into a society, it is quite possible Maistre belonged to one of those Masonic groups that prided themselves on being Martinists.

The potential effect of *L'Homme de désir* on a writer with Romantic inclinations is understood only after perusing its pages.

While Saint-Martin's text is obviously loaded with theosophic messages to the initiated, the book nonetheless impresses the reader as a work of substantial literary quality. Written in a clear and graceful style *L'Homme de désir* is patterned after the psalms, with a series of invocations to God and appeals to believers to enter into the mystical delights offered by Martinism. Attracted by the style of writers as well as their ideas Maistre read Saint-Martin unquestionably with equal appreciation of the literary merit and religious content of *L'Homme de désir.*

On the whole the message of *L'Homme de désir* is one of hope. Readers are enjoined to anticipate with pleasure the prospects of the afterlife: "Oh, how beautiful will be the reality of the future world in our eyes, because the illusion of this present world . . . is so imposing and so magnificent!"[33]

Passages such as the above must have instilled hope in Maistre and rendered him amenable to Saint-Martin's instructions on the attitude requisite for effective prayer to the Almighty. Comments in the *Soirées* on the role of prayer in man's spiritual life at times seem an echo of *L'Homme de désir:* "When your heart is full of God, use verbal prayer. . . . When your heart is dry and empty use silent and concentrated prayer. . . . It is one single resource . . . in this dark region and on this miserable stage of expiation."[34]

The proper objects of meditation for the initiated person who, through regeneration has truly become an *homme de désir,* are pure spirits or angels representing a higher level of Creation: "The regenerated man gazes without interruption on the pure and living beings whose appearance sanctifies him."[35] Closely related to the motif of regeneration so prominent in the *Soirées* is the concept of a primitive revelation, an idea that is clearly outlined for Maistre's consideration by Saint-Martin, who in all probability impressed upon the Count the importance of this truth for anyone who was a disciple of Martinism: "Have not irresistible proofs about the first truths already been manifested to the nations?"[36]

Unlike those possessing theosophic insights ordinary men rely on human laws to establish a social order. Ignorant of the true source of transcendent laws for mankind — which originated with the divine will manifesting itself to the hearts and minds of men, especially at the dawn of civilization — modern man tries in vain to set up a government based on fragile and ephemeral laws of his own making: "They still do not even know the origin of their political and terrestrial rights; however they are not in any less of a hurry to prescribe for themselves laws that they believe just as soon as their votes are counted."[37]

There remains one valid explanation for man's loss of the primitive revelation, namely, a grievous offense against God. The theme of original sin, so central to the *Soirées*, is firmly asserted by Saint-Martin in tracing the reasons for man's fall from grace: "Reflect on these irrefutable facts and deny, if you can, an original crime."[38]

The fact of a serious act committed in defiance of divine law suffices to explain the ease with which many men lapse into a life of sin. In stressing this sad aspect of the human condition Saint-Martin refers to the relations between the criminal and executioner in a passage that may have prompted Maistre to enlarge on the comparison and develop the striking symbolism presented so forcefully in the *Soirées:* "The criminal who has done nothing to the executioners could tell them that it is with injustice that they torment him, because he has done nothing to them; but he senses that it is with justice that he is sentenced to suffering and death."[39]

Just as Maistre in the *Soirées* finds the ultimate justification of the executioner's role in the need for sacrifice, so did Saint-Martin previously in *L'Homme de désir* outline the necessity of sacrifice in accomplishing the expiation required to atone for man's fall. Saint-Martin's charge to his disciples, similar to Maistre's subsequent consideration of the function of expiation, deals with the general responsibility of mankind and thus by implication involves the innocent as well as the guilty: "Were we to have sufferings in expiration? We were to have only sufferings in sacrifices; because charity alone was to animate all beings, and they were to have no other task than working for the reestablishment of the alliance."[40]

Saint-Martin is speaking of the restoration of the original union between God and man through mystical experience. One of the chief factors in the rupture of this fruitful relationship was the loss of the primitive revelation made to man through the gift of language bestowed on him by God. In this gift was contained the disclosure of man's purpose in the divine plan, the fact of his creation, and the laws God wished him to observe in establishing a society on earth. Saint-Martin states forcefully the divine origin of language and its inevitable corruption when reduced to written form: "The word had been necessary for the institution of the word. . . . Man had received this word; he had been chosen to be the singer of God and to celebrate all the wonders of his glory. . . . Would it then be true that it is by writing that languages have been lost? . . ."[41]

In view of Maistre's unremitting praise of Saint-Martin and the recapitulation in the *Soirées* in more detailed form of several themes central to *L'Homme de désir*, the relationship between the two works is clear and unmistakable. Of course Maistre could draw on other sources for the philosophical position formulated in the *Soirées*, but *L'Homme de désir* remains the primary source in terms of the literary inspiration exercised on Maistre as a creative writer. The imagery of the *Soirées* unquestionably owes much to the delicate phrasing of ideas in *L'Homme de désir*.

In this connection the broader influence of Saint-Martin on French Romanticism is closely linked with Maistre's publicizing the merits of *L'Homme de désir*. One of the poets to officially launch the Romantic movement in France utilized Martinist themes in his poetry; the *Méditations* of Lamartine had several passages strongly Martinist in flavor. The poet's friendship with Maistre had indubitably led to the former's introduction to Saint-Martin.[42] Since many Romantic writers read at least the *Soirées* they would, also, thanks to Maistre, learn of the "unknown philosopher."

Several of the commonplaces enunciated by French Romantic poets to stress the divine origins of their mission are traceable to *L'Homme de désir*, which in turn was indebted to Jacob Boehme and earlier theosophists. The French Romantics had an immediate source in Saint-Martin. Lamartine's concept of the poet, shared by his fellow writers, often seems a paraphrase of *L'Homme de désir* where Saint-Martin gives serious consideration to the role of the poet as a prophet: "But epic poetry cannot get along without prophetic poetry, the only poetry truly powerful and capable of providing for all the legitimate needs of our spirit. . . ."[43]

The theosophist's description of the function of his dedicated disciple, the *homme de désir*, apparently was adopted by French Romantics to apply to the sacerdotal role they assigned to the poet. Lamartine and Hugo both prided themselves on their hieratic office in the service of mankind: "Man of desire, go there alone like the great priest."[44]

Sainte-Beuve was tempted to trace Lamartine's lyric effusions to *L'Homme de désir* but did not press the inquiry far enough. Only in the present century has the extent of theosophic influences on French Romanticism been fully realized.[45] Besides Lamartine other writers like Nodier and Nerval underwent in varying degrees the spell of Saint-Martin. Baudelaire's exposure to Martinism through Maistre was no passing phase but an involved process. Treated too long as an intriguing but relatively minor figure, Saint-Martin merits serious consideration in any study of the underlying causes of French Romanticism.

CHAPTER 5

Miscellaneous Writings

BESIDES the *Soirées* Maistre produced a series of inciden-
tal writings on a variety of subjects. Some were composed prior
to his appointment to the Russian court while others were written
during his residence in Saint Petersburg. All throw further light on
his literary, religious, and philosophical interests. In this chapter
they are treated in the order in which they occur in the Vitte collection.

I   Eclaircissement sur les sacrifices

Man did not invent God but from the first acknowledged His existence and worshipped Him in song and dance. Being a rational
creature endowed with intelligence and will, man in general from
the dawn of civilization has sensed that in the eyes of God all
humans were guilty of some primordial transgression of divine law.
Another truth accepted already by early man was the distinction
between body and soul as two separate entities.

In the development of various world religions it was generally understood that atonement for sins could be made by an offering of
blood as a sacrifice. This symbolized a cleansing and regeneration of
the spirit. While animals were widely used for sacrifice it is evident
from studying ancient religions that human sacrifices were made at
an early stage. Contrary to the speculations of Voltaire the sacrifice
of human beings did not occur as an afterthought, or the logical
result of the initial offering of animal blood.

Maistre is caught in a quandary over the widespread practice
among ancient and modern religions of human sacrifice. Having
always asserted that ancient cultures were privy to a divine revelation common to all pre-Christian religions Maistre finds it difficult to
deny that human sacrifice at one time was demanded by God, brutal
as the practice may now seem. Since the coming of Christ, however,
such cruel immolations are no longer justifiable.

The supreme sacrifice, that of the innocent for the guilty, finds its ultimate example in the Redemption. Human sacrifices before Christ prefigured His death on the Cross. In modern times the necessity of sacrifice in blood is seen in the execution of the hapless Louis XVI by the guillotine and the omnipresent horror of war.

Maistre recapitulates arguments already presented in the *Soirées* on the function of sacrifice in religion. This preoccupation with the inevitability of the immolation of the innocent becomes a symbol in Maistre's mind of the frightful price demanded by God's justice to atone for original sin: "The victim was always burned in whole or in part, in order to attest that the natural punishment for crime was fire, and that the *substituted* flesh was burned in place of the *guilty flesh*. . . ."[1]

Signs of a pre-Romantic bent in Maistre are perceptible in his recreation of worship of the Almighty in ancient times: "Music, poetry, dance, in a word all the pleasing arts were called to the ceremonies of the ritual."[2] He also takes pains to remind readers of his love of literature with a reference to *Paradise Lost*: "Milton put beautiful verses into the mouth of Satan who howled about his degradation."[3]

One interesting aspect of the *Eclaircissement sur les sacrifices* is Maistre's insistence that life might well exist on other planets in the solar system. Any intelligent life found there could very well have been the recipient of a revelation quite different from that given to men on earth. In such moments Maistre ceases to be a hard-line conservative and sounds more like a latterday *philosophe*.

II   Sur les Délais de la justice divine

Sur les délais de la justice divine is a translation from the Latin of Plutarch. In his comments on Plutarch Maistre obviously cites the Roman writer to his own advantage. Plutarch is used to substantiate several Maistrean notions on God, religion, and sacrifice. At times Seneca is presented in a more favorable light than Plutarch who, in Maistre's opinion, often lacks sufficient knowledge about Roman customs. Nonetheless, on the whole, Maistre is favorably inclined toward Plutarch, a writer who ostensibly was familiar with Christianity and shared some of the Christian views on morality.

III   Examen de la philosophie de Bacon

Bacon's conception of the state of science in the sixteenth century is largely a figment of his own imagination as far as Maistre is concerned. As a scientist Bacon could not hold a candle to Galileo and was hopelessly inferior to Descartes. For that reason D'Alembert's praise of Bacon, together with Condillac's adulation, makes absolutely no sense to Maistre.

Bacon's theory of induction was invalid and had nothing new to offer, Maistre argues. At least Aristotle was honest in his observations, since he had only the barest rudiments of science with which to work. Bacon, however, like many modern philosophers, wanted to found a new sect and in giving induction such prominence started a school of thought that led to the whole concept of induction being distorted by Hume and other moderns. If words and ideas are confused, then so is the entire syllogism.

One of Maistre's chief objections to Bacon and those who support him is their failure to give due recognition to the contributions of the scholastics in the Middle Ages. Much that has been acclaimed as new since the Renaissance is in reality little more than a restatement of principles already demonstrated by Aquinas and others. In refuting Aristotle Bacon at the same time steals his ideas.

Appalled by Bacon's materialism, Maistre discovers even in the Englishman's style a frightening insensitivity to anything spiritual. How then, Maistre wonders, can Bacon speak of celestial causes when it is clear that an immaterial order has little meaning to him? Unable to distinguish between natural and supernatural truth Bacon rejects the notion that the marvels of the universe automatically lead man to seek God.

Hopelessly materialistic in outlook, Bacon is eminently unqualified to write on the soul and its functions. When he does, his exposition abounds in hypocrisy and sophistry. Nowhere does Bacon succeed in separating and clearly distinguishing the sensory and intellective operations of man's soul. In one instance Bacon juggles terms so clumsily that he has Moses saying that Jehovah created spirit but not matter. The evidence in Bacon's writing points overwhelmingly to a reluctance to admit the intervention of a divine agent in human affairs. Pascal, himself an accomplished scientist, had by contrast the humility to thank God for the air he breathed. By the same token Locke is decidedly inferior to Bossuet and Fénelon in his perception of God's hand in the universe. It is just as difficult to picture Locke or Bacon acknowledging the existence of God as it would be to imagine Rousseau preaching in a church pulpit.

Bacon's reputation in France is largely unwarranted, Maistre concludes, and is traceable to the Encyclopedia. He was the object of inordinate praise even though D'Alembert admitted most of the English philosopher's works were to a great extent unknown in France. Consequently, when Voltaire alludes mysteriously to a book by Bacon without identifying the work in question by title, Maistre is forced to conclude that Voltaire, like the rest of the *philosophes*, never read anything by Bacon.

Maistre's prime purpose in writing a devastating attack on Bacon was to continue the endless task of refuting the *philosophes* by undermining one of their idols. He is often unfair in his criticism and in his refusal to admit that Bacon may have made at least a few positive contributions. On the other hand, Maistre is not completely inaccurate in suggesting that the *philosophes* were guilty of lavish and uncritical praise. His defense of the scholastics and of the forgotten accomplishments of the Middle Ages also is a subject of considerable controversy, with much to be said in favor of the merits of the medieval schoolmen.

Of greater interest to readers today are Maistre's comments on Bacon as a writer. The Englishman, Maistre is willing to grant, was by instinct a creative writer: "Rarely does he resist the urge to be a poet."[4] Even with this taste for creativity Bacon lacks the makings of a great author; he is too materialistic in temperament, a propensity that betrays itself even in his writing:

His style, so to speak, is *material*; he exerts himself only on forms, on masses, on movements. His thought seems . . . *to become corporeal* and *to incorporate itself* with the objects that occupied him solely. . . . There is not in all his works one line, one word which addresses itself to the mind; *nature* or *essence* for example shock him; he prefers to say *form* because he sees it. . . .[5]

Bacon's materialism vitiates his style because, Maistre maintains, stylistic greatness is not achieved at the expense of eliminating all reference to the spiritual order. In analyzing Bacon's style Maistre also examines the Englishman's work in Latin, which he finds free of anglicisms but replete with gallicisms. Maistre concludes that if Bacon's style was harmed by sixteenth-century France the English philosopher amply repaid his French colleagues by becoming the source of much of the false and corrupt reasoning of the *philosophes*. But then such a development was unavoidable, for Bacon debased his own writing by unethically distorting the meaning of words, a trick that the *philosophes* were quick to learn and put into practice: "The charlatan is caught in a flagrant misdeed: *he changes the terms* — he wanted to teach us to look for the *essence*, and he talks to us about *qualities*. That is abusing language in order to deceive one's self and to deceive others. . . . What does this mess mean! . . ."[6]

After reflecting on Bacon's excessive misuse of language to spread errors and misinterpretations Maistre judges that the English author had little control over his proclivity to give a materialistic cast to his writing: "Each line of Bacon leads to materialism; but no where has he shown himself to be a more skilful sophist, a more refined hypocrite . . . than in what he has written on the soul."[7]

After struggling through Bacon's remarks on the soul Maistre is unable to refrain from heaping invective on his English opponent, a task which he undertakes with great relish and considerable verve in ridiculing Bacon's negligent use of terms: "Thus man is *light* and *fountain*, *will' o the wisp* and *torrent*. . . . Light is less brilliant, a will o' the wisp less subtle, a torrent less flowing than this eloquent tirade. . . ."[8]

Although Maistre clearly learned many lessons in satire and style from his reading of the *philosophes*, he always prefers to associate himself with the Classical writers of the seventeenth century, a period with a wholesome point of view. These qualities permeated the whole philosophy and outlook of its writers:

> It is still very important to notice that apart from the superiority of the seventeenth century in philosophical works properly speaking, its whole literature . . . breathes forth some intangible wise philosophy . . . which addressing itself constantly to universal common sense, surprises, shocks and disturbs no one. This exquisite tact, this perfect sense of proportion was named *timidity* by the following century which valued only contradiction, audacity and exaggeration. . . .[9]

Understandably, Maistre considered himself more at home with the writers of the era of Louis XIV and a supporter of their religious and political beliefs. While on the question of literary principles he also had much in common with them, the comparison does not obtain in all respects. Maistre, though he claimed to be an orthodox Christian steadfastly opposed to the *philosophes*, is more apt to give the impression to casual readers of his polemical writings that he was a lax Catholic well schooled in the Voltairean tradition of argumentation and satire. Besides being an unwilling heir of the Enlightenment he already betrayed some distinctly Romantic tendencies.

The rather prejudiced criticism of Bacon makes many of Maistre's judgments seem of little value. There is something to be said though for the remarks on Bacon's style. In attempting to explain the overall impression created by Bacon's choice of terminology Maistre touches briefly on stylistic and psychological factors that presumably affected the English writer in the act of composing a work. Unknowingly, Maistre stumbled upon some of the critical techniques that were to be developed in a far more sophisticated and complex manner during the twentieth century.

IV   Le caractère extérieur du Magistrat

Maistre's purpose in writing this treatise was to stress the integrity necessary for the maintenance of a magistrature that would deserve the public trust. His statements are consistent with the principles he has generally supported. The task of assuming the responsibility of government rests primarily with a ruling class, an hereditary aristocracy reared in the judicial tradition and anxious to observe the highest legal standards.

Addressing himself to fellow lawyers and judges Maistre reminds them that they are constantly in the public eye. They are judged by their silence as well as by their pronouncements. Bribery and collusion clearly have no place in an institution established for the common good. It is incumbent upon all judges to maintain absolute impartiality and not abandon the lofty position of the magistrate to engage in petty, partisan squabbles.

Le caractère extérieur du magistrat was originally an address delivered to the Senate of Savoy on December 1, 1784. From the treatise some insight is afforded into the thinking of Maistre in his formative years. His political orthodoxy is already clearly in evidence and the sincerity of his statements is substantiated by witnesses to the fairness of his own verdicts as a magistrate.

V   Lettres d'un royaliste savoisien *and the* Discours a Mme la marquise de Costa

The *Lettres d'un royaliste savoisien à ses Compatriotes* was printed in Lausanne in 1798. They cover a fairly wide range of subjects pertaining to the French invasion of Sardinia, the confiscation of the clergy's property, the forced exile of many aristocrats, and the *de facto* tyranny of a foreign army presumably sent to liberate an enslaved people. The foregoing points are called to the attention of the National Convention of France.

In five letters intended for fellow Sardinians Maistre examines the current tragic situation in their native land. Initially, Maistre tells his countrymen, the French Revolution appeared justified by the corruption that plagued the government. For a short while France was in the process of putting its house in order, unlike other decrepit courts in Europe. The salutary phase did not last long and was superseded by anarchy and chaos. Sardinians are warned to profit by the experience of the French and not abandon their king when the country is occupied by foreign troops. Revolutionary blandishments from French Republicans should not influence loyal Sardinians mindful of the actual tyranny in France — which stood in sharp contrast with the benign monarchy, the kind and compassionate clergy, and the just legal system under which they thrived and prospered.

In the midst of the dry rhetoric and stock political messages the more fervent and spontaneous side of Maistre is occasionally manifested. Very conscious of his French culture, he reminds the citizens of Savoy of their proud linguistic heritage, and with deep feeling speaks of the sacred foundations of Sardinia and all Christian governments: "Oh! holy and divine laws, celestial emanations! honor of human nature! It is only through you that Sovereigns approach their model. When one recollects an instant and reflects on the marvels of political organization one thinks he is hearing the voice of the Divinity itself. . . ."[10]

Rhetorical passages such as the above inject some warmth and color into Maistre's uniformly disciplined style in lesser works like the *Lettres d'un royaliste savoisien*. Noteworthy too is Maistre's admission that the French Revolution at least at the outset accomplished some positive changes by ushering in long needed reforms.

The *Discours à Madame la Marquise de Costa sur la vie et la mort de son fils Eugène*, written in 1794 and published posthumously, further laments the sad plight of Sardinia. Maistre's customary incisiveness is replaced by a heartfelt expression of sadness over the violence brought to a peaceful little kingdom and its people by a stronger nation. No Romantic writer could voice with deeper emotions Maistre's profound sense of loss: "Oh, my fatherland! Oh unfortunate people! How can you weep sufficiently for the dreadful neighboring country that has poured upon you a deluge of evils. A thousand times happier is the Laplander in the midst of his eternal ice! A thousand times happier the Bedouin Arab on his land *scorched* by a burning sun! . . ."[11]

In the years to come Maistre would seldom cry out with such unrestrained passion, since he became reconciled to exile and sought a long term solution for Europe's dilemma in a return to the Church and monarchy. Concealed beneath his biting attacks on revolution and rationalism was an intensely passionate nature that enabled him to persist in his mission.

VI Cinq Paradoxes

The *Cinq Paradoxes à Madame la Marquise de Nav*—, dated May 10, 1795, ostensibly were written at Turin. In reply to a letter from the Marquise, who recalls with delight the Count's explanation in a conversation of the usefulness of the paradox, Maistre proposes to illustrate his point more fully by considering five paradoxes in some detail.

The first paradox concerns dueling and to begin his discussion Maistre considers two solutions to the problem: "Rousseau, reasoning on this point, thought . . . in order to destroy duels it would be necessary to permit them. . . . Louis XIV . . . had conceived . . . his classification of impertinences . . . for the epithet of *Cad*, so many years in prison . . . for *coward* so many, etc. . . ."[12]

Maistre is not completely satisfied with either solution: "I would like to combine the two plans to form a third . . . the *nec plus ultra* of legislation."[13] Louis XIV's suggestion would be employed to draw up a list of insulting epithets that would make the user subject to the death penalty. When the guilty party was arraigned, the plaintiff with the judges' permission could be appointed an *ad hoc* executioner and thus enabled to legally slay his insulter. Maistre, always so meticulous about legal niceties, maliciously juxtaposes an arbitrary law, on one hand, and an atrociously legalized murder, on the other. Such was the cynical temperament formed by the backlash of the French Revolution.

The second paradox, that women are better suited than men to the governing of countries, has even deeper implications today in view of the growth of feminine liberation. With thinly veiled sarcasm Maistre calls attention to the fact that monarchies are governed by the rightful successor regardless of sex. Then assuming a tone he undoubtedly used quite frequently in the salon Maistre shrewdly and wittily analyzes a woman's qualifications for governing wisely and well. Flattery does not faze her since this appeals to her feminine nature without detracting from her ability to rule. Men can adjust easily to this situation: "Accustomed at an early stage to refuse nothing to a woman, to contradict her in no way, and to concede her everything, there is no reason to act otherwise because she is queen. . . ."[14]

There is only one catch to the theory of feminine superiority in governing countries. What is to be done if the monarch in time of war is expected to lead the army in person on the battlefield? As though foreseeing his eventual service in the court of the czar, Maistre adroitly cites the happy precedent set by Catherine the Great: "Certainly it is a very honorable spectacle for women, to see all the plans of Peter the Great, hatched by skirts, blossom majestically before the eyes of an astonished Europe. . . ."[15]

In the exposition of this second paradox Maistre displays impressively his ability to cater to feminine sensibilities and treat with a surprising lightness of touch such serious matters as the manner in which countries are governed in peace and war. His anglophilism manifests itself in the allusion to Elizabeth I as a prime example of a woman's success in ruling a nation.

The third paradox, that the most useful thing for men is game-playing, is used by Maistre to comment on the humorous situations in which people find themselves when engaged supposedly in a moment of relaxation. Such occasions can afford others the opportunity for amateur psychoanalysis. Take for example the cardplayer whose inner anxiety is betrayed by certain physical signs of nervousness: "What one calls the *character* of a man is only a collection of tics, and the tic is only a creature of habit."[16]

To end the third paradox Maistre presents an obnoxious example. A social climber, anxious to meet an influential aristocrat, simply views the whole affair as a game and writes a brazen letter to the nobleman stating his wish to meet him; in the letter he makes outrageous inquiries about the gentleman's family and personal affairs. Not satisfied with this effrontery the social-climber is prepared to carry the game one step further and meet his quarry in person. Maistre thus draws a thin line between frivolous games and the more serious ones played in the salon. He seems to ask the question, when does the game-playing cease and the political maneuvering commence?

The fourth paradox, that the notion of what is beautiful is based on convention and habit, begins with an excerpt from the letters of Mme de Sévigné in praise of the music of Lulli, a composer of only passing interest to concertgoers of Maistre's time. From Lulli's decline in popularity the Count is moved to comment on the age-old problem of permanence in aesthetic standards vis-a-vis the changing patterns of public taste. It is difficult to explain with any degree of objectivity how Lulli, applauded vigorously in his own day, suddenly faded into oblivion after his death. Since fickleness is so often a determining factor in judging beauty, current taste becomes an unreliable criterion of the aesthetic quality of things. Choosing a commonplace item Maistre remarks how the same beer will be displeasing on one occasion and on another quite appetizing and refreshing.

There are fields, Maistre facetiously observes, in which dogmas and principles of aesthetic judgment abound. Poetry is such a field, and even one or two lines become the source of furious controversy on the theme or on the choice of words necessary to give the desired effect and the versification. The last named subject is a particularly pesky one when it relates to French poetry. Maistre finds the rules on avoiding the clash of two vowel sounds in French rather arbitrary, especially when an additional letter is inserted to placate the rule-makers even though that letter remains unpronounced. Hairsplitting on rules and techniques, Maistre warns, often results in conflicting opinions on the aesthetic merits of a particular poem.

Another problem in the assessment of the beauty of a work of art, whether a play, a painting, or a statue, is the reliance of the viewer on the judgment of recognized critics. Opinions will change overnight if viewers discover their evaluation is in conflict with the decision of the critics. Maistre objects strongly to lavish praise of a painting seen for the first time, simply because it is well known that critics acclaim the painter as one of the best in Europe. Raphaël is admired because of his reputation, but he might well be neglected if ranked with secondary figures in art. Joshua Reynolds had little use for persons who heaped praise on one of Raphaël's paintings after having seen it only once. Maistre labels this type of aesthetic judgment a general sentiment, since it is based largely on commonplace feelings and attitudes with little or no effort to arrive at an original appraisal.

One solution to this dilemma is to assign the term beautiful to those works whose beauty can be fully appreciated only by a select few. Not satisfied even with this basis for determining which works are beautiful Maistre remarks that an opera is composed for a large audience and not six critics alone. The glaring abuses of limiting artistic appreciation to a clique of the initiated are forcefully demonstrated to Maistre by the position taken by Johann Winckelmann (1717 - 1768), the German art historian. Winckelmann's dictum, that ancient Greece was the sole period in history when art was truly dedicated to the expression of ideal beauty, was an assumption Maistre could not accept. The closed-minded followers of Winckelmann were easily duped, Maistre conjectures, by clever imitations of Greek statuary reproduced by unscrupulous sculptors and sold at exorbitant prices on the market.

Unconcerned about offending those who idolize Michelangelo, Maistre criticizes the Italian artist's portrayal of Moses. The statue of the biblical leader has the head of a satyr and is attired in butcher's garments, scarcely, Maistre protests, the interpretation befitting a great master. Michelangelo's depiction of Christ and the Virgin are hardly any better and oblige Maistre to dismiss the Italian's work as gross, exaggerated, and extravagant. In fact, much of the Italian Renaissance displeases Maistre because the movement failed to recapture the Greek ideal of beauty. Even Gothic art for all its imperfections retains a distinctive character. By this token the Renaissance in Italy as seen through the eyes of Maistre failed in its objective. The question of how to judge beauty, already sufficiently confused by the partisans of Winckelmann, is further complicated by those who countenance only European art, thereby excluding Asiatic masterpieces.

Another facet of the problem of making aesthetic judgments is the imitation of nature which Maistre refuses to interpret as the mere reproduction of an object; in any imitation of nature three points must be decided before hand, namely, what aspect of nature is to be imitated, to what degree the imitation must be realized, and the manner in which the imitation is accomplished. Maistre indicates that the color techniques used by Claude Lorrain and Jacob Ruysdael in depicting pastoral scenes meet with his approval, although the three points he prescribes cause considerable disagreement among the critics. Winckelmann's thesis that a positive idea of beauty can only be obtained through a knowledge of the essence of the beautiful merely intensifies the paradox in Maistre's mind. In order to decide what is beautiful we must refer to a previously established concept of beauty. Thoroughly perplexed by now, Maistre abandons his fourth paradox with a sign of relief.

The fifth paradox, that the reputation of books does not depend on their merit, is a somewhat humorous extension of the fourth paradox and deals with the at times rather mercurial standards by which books are judged. Here Maistre is unable to resist the temptation to cite books he personally opposes on religious and philosophical grounds. Pascal's *Lettres provinciales* would have failed if its inaccuracies were directed against the Capuchins instead of the Jesuits. In France and England the *Esprit des lois* received considerable praise, much of it justified, although specialists could penetrate Montesquieu's brilliant style to discover not a few errors in judg-

ment. Locke's *Essay Concerning Human Understanding* continued
to enhance an undeserved reputation for the author, simply because
the book was no longer read!

The prejudices that help a book achieve lasting acclaim often work
in favor of nations as well. The Chinese represent their country on
the map as a large land mass surrounded by small, insignificant
neighbors. In the same vein Frenchmen have an unwarranted es-
timate of their own cultural preeminence in picturing Paris and
France as the center of the universe. Outside of France that opinion
in strongly rejected.

Solid evidence convincing to Maistre can be adduced to substantiate the reputation of England's two great poets, Milton and
Shakespeare. Whether or not they surpass the eminent writers of ancient Greece is another matter; Addison made such a comparison in
the case of Milton to attract attention. As a result Milton is admired
although Maistre suspects few persons in the British Isles have read
Paradise Lost. Shakespeare is better known because he was a
playwright. Theatergoers, after all, outnumber by far those persons
who read long epic poems in the solitude of their parlors. What Dr.
Johnson says about the irregular features of the beauty characteristic
of Shakespeare's dramas is in sharp contrast to the uniformity partisans of French Classicism admire in Racine. The superb French
writer of tragedy parallels the Greek dramatists in several respects,
but although the English critics rate Greek theater over
Shakespeare's plays they refuse to admit any comparison between
Racine and Shakespeare. Such literary chauvinism causes Maistre to
remark, "This theorem of *trigonometry does not shock at all the
most discerning minds of Europe.*"[17]

In general Maistre accepts the critical judgment of Dr. Johnson
concerning Shakespeare and, forgetting his usual espousal of French
Classicism for a moment, praises the Bard of Avon unequivocally:
"Other poets painted an ideal nature. Shakespeare alone depicted a
true nature, a general nature, in a word, a *natural* nature."[18]

Leaving Shakespeare Maistre proceeds to subjects less agreeable
to him. Voltaire's epic poem, the *Henriade*, is a work which the
Count grudgingly concedes has some merit. But then, Maistre asks,
what constitutes true literary achievement? Richardson's *Clarissa
Harlowe*, the object of mixed reactions in England, was lauded
profusely in France by Diderot — for what reasons Maistre is at a
loss to explain. If the reader were to put aside all preconceived
notions a more dispassionate view of *Clarissa Harlowe* would be

possible. Then one glaring flaw of the novel could be readily detected, namely, the representation of vice as an attractive diversion. Nothing was more illogical than the portrayal of the villainous Lovelace as a forceful, energetic person in contrast to the virtuous though bungling Hyckman. The conclusion of the novel with Clarissa's refusal to marry is definitely not true to life, observes Maistre, with a Classicist's eye for *invraisemblance*; actually, the whole novel is an affront to the English nation and character.

Maistre terminates the fifth paradox on an appropriately ambiguous note by implying that it is foolish to assume that either a small select minority or an overwhelming majority has the final word in judging what is beautiful and what is not: "It is clear that all questions of taste must be decided . . . by the plurality."[19] Maistre preserves the mood of perplexity occasioned by the paradox by refusing to state precisely how the plurality arrives at its presumably valid judgment.

The five paradoxes treated by Maistre admit of different meanings. In the first paradox there is a proposition contrary to accepted opinion. Dueling was in most countries a crime during Maistre's lifetime, although he resorts to a cynical circumvention of the law to produce a sort of legalized duel. Perhaps Maistre was emphasizing the extent to which some individuals winked at the law when violating its spirit although outwardly obeying the letter.

Male chauvinists would be bound to find the second paradox rather offensive, with its statement that women were better rulers than men. The premise, nonetheless, seems reasonable when the reigns of Elizabeth of England and Catherine the Great of Russia are recalled. From an acceptable premise Maistre draws a seemingly valid conclusion to the effect feminine wiles enable women to assert their superiority in governing nations. But a contradiction is slipped into one of the consequences of the conclusion. If the nation is at war will a queen lead the troops into battle? Maistre begs the question by slyly referring to Catherine's success in carrying out the grand designs of Peter the Great. Nothing is said about her capacity to command soldiers on the battlefield.

The third paradox at first glance appears to be contrary to common sense. Men should presumably find something more useful to do than playing games. Yet Maistre, by his adroit application of the dictum, demonstrates that playing games in the broadest sense is a fact of everyday life for the hardened diplomat and leads to brazen courses of action.

In the case of the fourth paradox the Count applies the same principle used in the second paradox on feminine superiority in the governing of countries. Once more Maistre employs an acceptable premise — judging what is beautiful is based on habit and convention — to arrive at an apparently valid deduction that a plurality of cultured people can establish aesthetic standards; since their judgments reflect contemporary attitudes it follows that a work of art is considered beautiful if it conforms to current tastes and customs. But Maistre does not come to this conclusion without encountering some tantalizing obstacles. The whole question of taste is fraught with contradictions, and any attempt to legislate precise standards for beauty ends in the tyranny of a snobbish elite. Conversely, to follow a majority opinion in determining the aesthetic qualities of a work of art would result in utter chaos. Maistre does little to clear up the confusion in readers' minds; he refers vaguely to the decision of a plurality as the final determining factor in judging beauty. He furnishes no constructive proposal for coping with some very troublesome difficulties, problems that obviously remain unaffected by semantic subterfuges.

The reputation of books does not depend on their merit, Maistre coyly suggests, in the hope of teasing readers with another question frequently the source of much controversy. How can a book devoid of intrinsic worth enjoy any reputation whatsoever? Here Maistre does not hesitate to speak as the fiery polemicist and excoriate his philosophical adversaries. Writers like Locke had substantial reputations largely unwarranted in view of the deleterious contents of their books — highly publicized but seldom read. As for novels Maistre picks an English book extremely popular in France but otherwise of little value: Richardson's *Clarissa Harlowe* is dismissed by the Count as an inferior work owing to immoral elements in its plot and climax. The fifth paradox for Maistre is the one found most commonly in the everyday world.

In selecting the five paradoxes to be treated Maistre chooses examples drawn from his own experience. Questions arising from dueling, the qualifications of women for ruling, and game-playing would be frequent topics of conversation in the salon when participants were in a gay and frivolous mood. More serious in nature were the problems associated with the standards for aesthetic judgments and the criteria for assuring the lasting reputation of a book. The general nature of the paradoxes and Maistre's discussion of them provide some useful insights into his own perception of the people and institutions with which he dealt everyday. His views on the implications of dueling, games, and feminine rulers are readily understandable in light of the confused state of the society in which he lived. The two paradoxes dealing with literary and artistic matters are of greater value and shed considerable light on Maistre's own aesthetic opinions and principles.

It is apparent that Maistre was on the whole more broad-minded than generally believed, at least in matters pertaining to culture and the arts. He is ready to concede that the omission of China and Asia in general from any comparative study of civilizations is an unpardonable oversight. Unlike other fellow writers in France he appreciated the genius of Milton and Shakespeare without abandoning his own essentially Classical position evidenced both in his praise of Racine and in his comments on the imitation of nature. Even on the latter question he shows that his ideas were in a state of transition and not locked in a tight unyielding interpretation of nature and its place in art. On the subject of establishing criteria for assessing the beauty of a work Maistre anticipates the abuses of esoteric modern schools; he rejects the concept of artistic standards fixed by an elite clique. While shunning the anarchy of a majority voice deciding aesthetic questions Maistre is ready to accept the judgment of a fair-sized minority of cultivated persons. For all practical purposes Maistre was manifesting already definite, even if limited, signs of Romantic tendencies. Only when criticizing the illicit love in *Clarissa Harlowe* does he disassociate himself from the general current of pre-Romanticism.

VII *Writings Against the Revolution*

Two short tracts, the *Addresse du Maire de Montagnole à ses concitoyens* (1795) and the *Discours du Citoyen Cherchemot* (1799), represent Maistre's efforts in the field of political pamphleteering. Both tracts were designed to ridicule the revolutionary government in France and encourage Sardinians to remain loyal to their king. The *Bienfaits de la Révolution Française*, also written in the 1790s and in a similar vein, is a longer satire on the government in Paris. Maistre goes into some detail in deriding the alleged accomplishments of the proletarian regime; he outlines its failure to cope adequately with problems on all levels, foreign, domestic, social, economic, and cultural.

In Maistre's estimation, the most unforgivable offense committed by the revolutionists was the damage done to the arts in

France — damage from which the nation would not soon recover: "Not only did the Revolution strike a perceptible blow to art by destroying or exiling an infinite number of masterworks in all fields, it gave them a still deeper wound by the type of men brought to power and influence. . . ."[20] Maistre was correct in ascribing the decline of the arts to the action of the revolutionary government. With a few notable exceptions, the general dearth of talent and productivity during the Revolution and the Empire attests to the validity of Maistre's charges.

Son Em. le Cardinal Maury, written in Venice in 1799, is a brief description of a visit paid to a prelate who had been in the early days of the National Assembly a fiery defender of the Bourbons and the object of scurrilous attacks in revolutionary pamphlets. Maistre's account of his visit to the Cardinal is a record of a calmer period in Maury's life after narrowly escaping the guillotine.

The *Examen d'un écrit de J.-J. Rousseau sur l'inégalité des conditions* provides Maistre with another opportunity to assail the *Vicaire Savoyard*. Not content with the blistering assault on Jean-Jacques in the *Soirées*, Maistre, with great gusto, recapitulates his main objections to Rousseau's philosophical and political views. The question on the origin of social inequality proposed by the Academy of Dijon was, Maistre derisively concedes, tailor-made for a maladjusted writer: ". . . Rousseau seized upon this subject designed expressly for him. Everything that was obscure, everything that presented no definite meaning, everything that lent [itself] to digressions and equivocations were especially in his field."[21]

Maistre replies to Rousseau's arguments by utilizing the empirical method so dear to the *philosophes*. From all reports private property was an institution of long standing among remote tribes in Asia and, Rousseau's protestations notwithstanding, the American Indians in their less attractive moments were not simple children of nature but bloodthirsty savages. When Rousseau spoke of an ideal state of nature it could be, Maistre points out, one of several states, none of which corresponds to Jean-Jacques' vague and unfounded suppositions.

By referring to known examples of savage people, Maistre is often on firm ground in challenging the assumptions of Rousseau concerning the noble savage. The Count has a positive attitude in indicating that supposedly primitive tribes have, in reality, a degree of civilization, a mark of intelligence which Maistre deems natural to all men. Recent anthropological studies have revealed the wide diversity among primitive tribes, few of which approximate Rousseau's description. Maistre's comments on the American Indian are, on the basis of current knowledge, no less far-fetched than those of Rousseau.

VIII   Letters de Mme de Sévigné

The *Observations critiques sur une édition des Lettres de Mme de Sévigné* was written about 1806 and first published in the Vitte collection. Maistre's comments concerned an edition of the *Letters* under the editorship of a M. Grouvelle, a self-styled ex-legislator. The Count was thus prejudiced beforehand by two facts, a chronic suspicion he entertained about any eighteenth-century criticism of a writer of the *ancien régime* and the term ex-legislator. The latter suggested Grouvelle was a constitutionalist — tantamount to waving a red flag before a bull in the negative impression it gave to Maistre.

Enraged at the outset by Grouvelle's labeling Mme de Sévigné a freethinker, Maistre takes him to task for assuming the slightest criticism by her of Catholic practices constituted a definitive rejection of Church teachings. But then the Count did not expect a *philosophe* and ex-legislator to arrive at a true and factual analysis. Maistre concluded that the anticlericalism of Grouvelle caused him to attack automatically any friends or acquaintances of Mme de Sévigné.

Already a prime target for the *philosophes*, Bossuet was, Maistre protests, calumniated by Grouvelle along with other figures who were either converts to Catholicism or faithful practitioners of its precepts. Most absurd of all in Maistre's eyes was Grouvelle's attempts to distort Bossuet's attitude toward Rome and to question the sincerity of the archbishop's efforts to woo Protestants back into the fold. The Count furiously denies Grouvelle's allegations of casuistry and duplicity on the part of Bossuet.

Conservative as Maistre is in his views on woman's traditional place in society, he sounds like an exponent of feminine liberation by comparison to Grouvelle, who apparently felt Mme de Sévgné had contributed little if anything to French letters. Maistre finds Grouvelle's statement that women never have had the ability to produce great works of art preposterous and refers to the poetry of Sapho, whose immorality may shock the Count but does not affect his ability to appreciate her genius.

Grouvelle's format for the edition of Mme de Sévigné's letters is mercilessly scrutinized and ridiculed by Maistre. A bungling and arbitrary arrangement of the text in chronological order deprived readers of a logical presentation of her most significant correspondence with important figures. The footnoting and textual commentaries were also extraordinarily awkward. To Maistre's amusement Grouvelle's work merely provided readers with insights into his own egregious shortcomings as a writer instead of furnishing a significant edition of Mme de Sévigné's letters with details that offered a fresh view of the author.

Despite Maistre's patent bias his criticism of Grouvelle is in the main warranted. Mindful of Voltaire's denigration of Pascal, Maistre was especially sensitive about any criticism of seventeenth-century writers by a *philosophe*, and, to a certain extent, his supicions of Grouvelle are justified by the latter's obvious attempts to transform Mme de Sévigné into an incisive *esprit fort*, a freethinker in the best traditions of the Enlightenment.

Of more than passing interest are Maistre's remarks on Grouvelle's ostensibly pedestrian and awkward style. "The editor possesses a marvelous talent for combining constantly a barbarism with an erroneous thought," fulminates the Count. "M. Grouvelle is the first man without taste and without talent, the first detestable writer we have seen take an enthusiastic interest in these letters."[22]

Maistre maintains that good style must express ideas truthfully and logically, a quality decidedly lacking in Grouvelle: "One would say that he always has next to him a malicious fairy who whispers to him the most outlandish expressions."[23] Whenever the time would come that a man's writings did not suffice to judge him, then M. Grouvelle might be considered a great figure, but only, Maistre warns, in that very unlikely eventuality.

From Maistre's criticism of Grouvelle substantial evidence can be adduced of his capacity for literary criticism. In spite of fixed opinions he was quite capable of objectively evaluating a work, and he had a sufficient acquaintance with literature in general to make substantive comments on a variety of authors and genres. Diplomatic affairs absorbed much of his time and only in casual writings is there any indication of his potential as a literary critic.

IX Incidental Writings on Religious Subjects

The *Réflexions sur le Protestantisme dans ses rapports avec la souveraineté* was written in 1798 and published in the Vitte edition. This treatise was composed by Maistre in one of his most dogmatic and reactionary moods. Protestantism, he averred, was conceived in rebellion, and insurrection was its natural condition. Never was any action more necessary and defensible than the Edict of Nantes whereby Louis XIV expelled the Huguenots. The Protestants with their unrestricted freedom in interpreting the Bible were a constant source of sedition and revolt. In his attack on Protestantism Maistre is primarily concerned with its manifestation in France. Possibly he was offended by the French revolutionary government's granting equal status to all religions and the active participation of certain Huguenots in the National Assembly.

The *Lettres à Jean Potocki sur la chronologie biblique* were written in 1810 and first appeared in the *Lettres et Opuscules* in 1851. A discussion of biblical chronology provides an excuse for another polemical outburst. Here the rationalists' criticism of the Bible comes under Maistre's fire. Whereas Protestants accepted the divine inspiration of Scripture but interpreted it without license, the *philosophes* did everything in their power to destroy the credibility of the Bible. The particular phase of the *philosophes'* criticism that infuriated Maistre was their questioning of biblical chronology. If the arrangement of data in order of time was accepted in the sacred books of the Chinese and Hindus then why doubt the chronology of Scripture? To be valid any chronological table had to correct false dates and furnish fresh proof of the validity of dates already accepted as true.

In reality, Maistre observes, the *philosophes* are guilty of the naiveté they attribute to Catholic exegetes; the rationalists of the eighteenth century deny what exists and explain what does not exist. Their notion of what the Bible meant by the flood, by way of example, was so ridiculous that the whole earth by their calculations would be inundated. Catholic interpretation was not so extravagant; it conjectured that the flood spoken of in Scripture applied to a relatively small area of the then known world. In this respect Maistre was on fairly firm ground, for archaeology was a budding science and the *philosophes* often made gratuitous and unsubstantiated assumptions.

Further exercises in Catholic apologetics are contained in the *Lettres à une dame protestante et à une dame russe.* In the first letter a Protestant lady is informed in no uncertain terms about the errors of the Reformation; in the second a member of the Russian Orthodox Church is warned of the heresies inherent in her religion. By its own utterances on the origins of ecclesiastical authority the Russian Church has tacitly admitted the supremacy of Rome. Maistre argues the various points in his usual clear and pithy, if somewhat obstinate and authoritarian, style.

Trois Opuscules sur l'éducation publique en Russie provides a glimpse of Maistre's ideas on education. As to be expected, the Jesuits are defended and the classical languages stressed as the essential foundation of sound instruction in the humanities. There is a stern warning from the Count to avoid the teaching of French rationalism and German illuminism. Physical and biological sciences, too closely associated with the Enlightenment, are dismissed as frills along with history, a subject best mastered by voluminous reading on the student's own.

The *Observations sur le Prospectus Disciplinarum ou plan d'études, proposé pour le séminaire de Newski par le professeur Fessler* is largely a summary of Kant's philosophy. Maistre scoffs at man's inability to prove by reason the existence of God with any degree of certainty and wearily assigns Kant's highly publicized metaphysics to the category of another run-of-the-mill system of German transcendentalism. He ends the treatise with a warning against Ignaz Fessler's mixture of Kantianism, Platonism, and Christianity.

The *Mémoire sur la liberté de l'enseignement public* is largely a review of the opinions expressed in *Trois Opuscules. Quatre chapitres sur la Russie* treats of liberty, science, religion, and illuminism in their relationship to Russia. Maistre underlines the part played by Christianity in suppressing slavery while at the same time acknowledging that serfdom was necessary under certain conditions. Countries were usually governed by a religious principle, even non-Christian nations like Turkey and China. Russia, unfortunately, had been contaminated in the eighteenth century by the writings of the *philosophes*. As a safeguard against the encroachment of scientism on religion in Russia, Maistre proposes a policy of preventing scientific academies from overstepping their bounds; he wishes to have science develop within defined limits, without any interference from the Czar's administration. Once more the Count admonishes Russians to beware of Protestantism and the heretical forms of illuminism devoid of the divine insights provided by Masonry and Martinism. Too often illuminists permitted their beliefs to become decadent and revolutionary. After urging a reconciliation between Catholicism and the Russian Church Maistre terminates his argument: "All that has been said is founded on experience, on the intimate knowledge of men, of the age, of circumstances, and of

Russia in particular. Each assertion is supported by unimpeachable witness, all wrested from the accused by the *torture of the truth.*"[24]

In a further attempt to demonstrate the ease with which the Western and Eastern Churches can be reunited Maistre examines several theological points to show the extent to which Methodius agreed with Rome. The *Reflexions critiques d'un chrétien dévoué à la Russie, sur l'ouvrage de Méthode, archevêque de Twer* was originally written in Latin and subsequently translated into French. By writing in Latin Maistre obviously hoped to reach theologians throughout Europe.

Two other essays, the *Discours pour le retòur du roi de Sardaigne dans ses états de terre ferme* and the *Lettres à M. le Marquis . . . sur la fête séculaire des protestants,* concern, respectively, the rights of the King of Sardinia and the bad effects of the Reformation on the Church.

Further objections to the spread of Protestant teaching through the Bible Society are voiced in the *Lettres à M. le Marquis . . . sur l'état du Christianisme en Europe:* "The French Revolution was only a direct consequence, a visible and inevitable conclusion of the principles posed in the sixteenth and eighteenth centuries; and now the state of Europe is such that it leaves one to still fear the most violent convulsions."[25] The Bible Society attacked by Maistre could have been one of two organizations, or he may have placed both under one label. Bible groups were active both in Switzerland and England to provide cheap editions of the Scriptures. Maistre's inclusion of the Reformation and the French Revolution in the same movement of protest is a logical classification and one adopted by some historians. He had an instinctive fear of all challenges to Church and royal authority, and in his usual apocalyptic vision he foresaw considerable bloodshed and suffering of the innocent to satisfy the demands of God's justice.

CHAPTER 6

Correspondence

MAISTRE'S correspondence did not appear in a substantive edition until about thirty years after his death. The first important edition was published in 1851 by his son, Rodolphe, at Vaton in Paris. The Vitte edition appeared with six volumes of correspondence between 1884 and 1887, and includes most of the letters written by Maistre. They furnish an ample amount of material for the student; specialized researchers also consult sources like the Vorontsov Archives and Albert Blanc's collection of Maistre's political correspondence published in 1858.

Letters written by Maistre from 1786 to 1821 begin with those composed in a relaxed mood at Chambéry and conduct the reader through the French invasion of Sardinia, the long period at the Russian court, and finally the return to Savoy where he spent his last years. In general the style reveals the author's usual alertness and attentiveness to detail. While having the customary Maistrean clarity the letters are frequently more casual and familiar in tone. The range of subjects covered embraces diplomacy, historical events, and personal observations on a wide variety of topics literary and philosophical. One letter written at Chambéry in 1786 sets forth the Count's views on the theater.

I *Letters of Early Period*

A certain actress, Mlle Saint-Val, elicits some incisive remarks from Maistre on her inept acting and overrated ability: "I found her reputation prodigiously exaggerated like everything which comes from France."[1] Some of her mannerisms, designed to register shock and surprise, displeased the Count, who admits she performs tolerably well in plays by secondary dramatists but remains unequal to the challenge of Corneille and Racine. Some features of her technique he could abide; other aspects of her emoting left him cold. Even though his correspondent was an in-law of Mlle Saint-Val, Maistre expresses his views quite bluntly:

The harsh poets are precisely those she renders the best. She does not know how to declaim Racine; she renders Voltaire better, because he is more sententious and less natural. She has given us nothing of Corneille or Crébillon, because apparently these little writers are not worthy of her talent. . . . In spite of all these drawbacks, your sister-in-law can pass for a great actress, provided she does not move out of her category. She expresses fury, jealousy, despair very well, in a word all the passionate and heartrending feelings, one must only warn her not to be carried away, for she shouts and tires the ear. . . . The cry that she uttered when she recognized Raoul . . . was that of nature, and it still resounds in my ear; finally she gave me an idea of perfection. . . . Conclusion: her talent is great, but mixed with great shortcomings. . . .[2]

Maistre's evaluation of Mlle Saint-Val covers the principal facets of her dramatic style, voice, manner, gesticulations, and interpretation of various dramatists. Ostensibly, Maistre either had been reading Diderot or readily recalled passages of the *Neveu de Rameau*. The allusion to the "cry of nature," evidently taken from Diderot's work, is significant inasmuch as it places Maistre with those critics whose assessment of the drama already reflected a Romantic attitude toward the theater and acting. While still a strong partisan of the Classical stage Maistre seemingly was attracted to Diderot's dramatic theories and preferred a style of acting with more emphasis on emotional tone.

In a more humorous vein Maistre tells his sister Thérèse about his bouts with the colic and then proceeds to trace the cause of his physical distress to the serpent in the Garden of Eden who refused to eat the apple in preference to victimizing Adam and Eve. Through a rather abrupt transition he passes from the scene of the Original Sin to Saint-Martin's *Homme de désir*. Thérèse has reservations about the validity of some points in Saint-Martin's work but Maistre, already a supporter of the theosophist, is not willing to accept his sister's criticism: "I endeavor to uphold his orthodoxy over all the leaders, even the National Assembly, which he clearly condemns."[3]

Terrifying events in Europe elicit from Maistre rather melodramatic observations on the existing state of affairs. The execution of Louis XVI evokes a comparison with English treatment of Charles I. Maistre, who always considered the revolt in England legal and valid, perceived nothing exceptionable in the conduct of Cromwell:

What a century, good God, or to put it better, what a nation! Compare the conduct of the English toward the unfortunate Charles I; you will see that the French are inferior to their rivals in crimes as well as in great deeds, and that the first nation is to the second . . . what the hyena is to the lion.[4]

Maistre makes an analysis here of the Revolution for the Comte de Beauregard, a close family friend. The allusion to Cromwell is noteworthy, foreshadowing as it does the fascination of French Romantics with the somber leader of the English rebels. Vigny, Hugo, Lamartine, and others judged Cromwell one of the truly puzzling and mysterious figures in European history.

Letter-writing was without question an enjoyable pastime for Maistre; he fills his correspondence with vivid details on military maneuvers and skirmishes during the French invasion of Savoy. At times, he confesses to the Baron Vignet des Etoles, letter-writing threatens to keep him from finishing the *Essai sur la Souveraineté*: "My correspondence alone is becoming an immense work."[5]

His resignation to a streak of bad luck won him the compliments of Count Coconato, although Maistre was unwilling to concede anything unusual in his personal outlook on the sorry state of affairs in Europe: "I do not accept the compliment that you give me on my philosophy. What we call by this fine name is most often only a basic frame of mind. In me it can only be a little of this Gallic genius which at times disconcerts misfortune by laughing in its face. . . ."[6]

If Maistre could react to the crisis on the continent with a studied cynicism he could with equal facility relax sufficiently to chuckle with enthusiasm at the efforts of his daughter, Constance, to have the details of *Télémaque* at the tip of her fingers and to tease her about being frightened when Fénelon had Mentor toss the hapless Télémaque headfirst into the water. News that his child was improving her mind by reading a solid work by one of the great Classical writers delighted him no end.

Proud as he was of the Classical tradition in French literature the Count also had a decidedly Romantic penchant for glorifying historical figures; he exhibited an unmistakable nostalgia, in the manner of a novelist of the Walter Scott school. "The French Bourbons are certainly not inferior to any ruling race; they have much spirit and goodness," asserts Maistre; the Bourbons gave France a strong government even though at present they were "in no way

capable of reestablishing it."[7] For that reason Maistre, with his un-
predictable view of history, singles out Napoleon as the man,
divinely selected perhaps, to restore the rightful monarchy: "I think
myself then well justified in believing that the commission of
Bonaparte is to reestablish the monarchy, and to open all eyes,
irritating equally the royalists and Jacobins, after which he will disappear. . . ."[8] Maistre's ability to read into events about him an
almost preternatural significance sets him apart from the matter-of-
fact commentators on political developments. His idealized conception of the Bourbons and even of Napoleon's role, in a period of transition, imparts a flavor and color to history that was to typify Romantic novelists like Vigny and Dumas *père*, who glossed over the sordid
details of human events to present a glowing account of heroic persons and deeds.

Some of Maistre's capacity for giving an ideal form to individuals
and incidents may derive from his reading of Homer and Tasso.
Swapping quotations from Homer with his daughter Adèle, he teases
her about not using a good translation. Maistre is inwardly pleased
by her choice of reading: "I praise very much your taste for Tasso.
. . . *Jerusalem Delivered* will always be one of the great masterworks
of modern genius."[9] Like many distinguished authors, he tells his
daughter, Tasso had flaws in technique and style, and Boileau was in
a measure correct in pointing them out; Maistre admits Boileau's
criticism of Tasso has some value, but he refuses to be the inflexible
French Classicist in relegating Tasso to the position of a minor
writer.

The Count's continued interest in his daughter's preferences in
authors and literature afforded him some relief from the dreary
hours spent in diplomacy and politics. From him Adèle receives
strict orders to supervise the reading of her brother Rodolphe in the
French poets: "Let him get them into his head, especially the inimitable Racine, no matter if he does not understand them yet."[10] If
Maistre could fall asleep while his mother read aloud from Molière,
it was incumbent on his own offspring to perpetuate the family tradition of appreciating the Classical writers. In fact, Adèle would do
well, he observes, to peruse carefully the *Femmes savantes* of
Molière:

Do you think this great writer of comedy, this infallible judge of ridiculous
people would have treated this subject, if he had not recognized that the title of learned women is in effect a ridiculous one? The greatest shortcoming
for a woman is to be a man. In order to do away even with the idea of this

unfavorable pretention, one must absolutely obey Solomon, Fénelon, and Molière; this trio is infallible. . . .[11]

Maistre goes on to assure Adèle that in keeping with Molièje's advice, she will be more intriguing in men's eyes if they first observe her sewing and knitting like a paragon of feminine submissiveness — only to discover later she is conversant with Klopstock and Tasso. The Count himself obviously failed to profit by more complimentary portraits of sensible and strong-minded women in other comedies by Molière. Mme Jourdain may not have been well read, but she was not subservient by any means to masculine ego. Maistre's rather odd version of male chauvinism probably explains his reaction to an illustrious contemporary, Mme de Staël. Her struggle against Napoleon did not change the Count's opinion of her. When writing to one of his many social acquaintances, the Marquise de Priero, about a recent party they both attended, he reminds her facetiously of the celebrity with whom she went for a stroll:

> You are the one . . . who went walking with *Knowledge in skirts*! I congratulate you, and I am delighted you could, like me, examine closely this celebrated, or notorious, lady who could have been adorable, and who only wished to be extraordinary. One must not argue about tastes, but according to mine she is mistaken. . . . She says very well what she wants to say. I do not know any head so completely perverted. It is the infallible operation of modern philosophy on any woman whatsoever, but her heart is not bad at all. In this respect, people have done her an injustice. As for intelligence, she has it in abundance, especially . . . when she does not seek to have any. Not having studied theology or politics together we created scenes in Switzerland that would make you die laughing, however, without ever getting into a serious argument. . . .[12]

Reminiscing further about Mme de Staël Maistre makes it clear that substantial disagreement on religion and philosophy did not interfere with a warm personal relationship he had with Mme de Staël and her family. The arch-apologist of royalism and Catholicism debated wittily and dispassionately with the leading spokesman for liberal Protestantism and a more republican trend in literature. An interesting insight is provided here into the tolerance and restraint Maistre exercised in personal contacts—in sharp contrast with the aspersions cast on hostile ideologies in his writings.

The opportunity to recall encounters with Mme de Staël and other celebrities in the salon must have provided Maistre with a welcome breathing spell, since the mental stress caused by the Napoleonic wars usually tasked his inner resources severely as he admitted to a friend: "I confess to you that there arises in my heart certain reactions that make me waver, despite the absolute determination of reason. I say to myself, like Montaigne, what do I know? Such extraordinary events occur. . . ."[13] The complexity and unpredictability of the international situation momentarily turned the usually devout Catholic into an agonizing cynic, fearful of Napoleon's next move.

Maistre's dilemma was further complicated by divided loyalties. Profoundly French by reason of language and culture he nonetheless remained faithful to the king of Sardinia, although the disillusion caused by the country's collapse before the French troops resulted in personal antipathy for the Sardinian populace: "They are cowards without obedience, and rebels without courage. They have studies without science, jurisprudence without justice, and worship without religion. . . . The Sardinian is more savage than the savage, for the savage does not know the light and the Sardinian hates it. . . ."[14]

II   *Period of Solitude in Russia*

The bitterness Maistre felt about the events that separated him from his family and imposed a virtual exile in a cold and distant Russia was reflected in his letters. He complained to his king, Victor-Emmanuel, about the loneliness far away from loved ones; even in the midst of practically interminable accounts of battles and diplomatic intrigues he would occasionally note briefly and pathetically the pains and anguish of solitude. In 1808, he was at the nadir of despair when Russia signed a pact with France. The treaty was a de facto recognition of the French conquest of Sardinia.

"National hatreds produce only evil,"[15] he sadly observes in a *mémoire* of 1806. Nothing appeared to have been accomplished by the wars against Napoleon. The governments of the German states were infected by French rationalism and a vicious form of illuminism. Resignation to impending disaster was an axiom of the day Maistre gloomily accepted: "Every man who does not place his death in the order of possible events, has not made great progress in philosophy." Proud of his intellectual achievements and reputation for cool analysis Maistre still rejects detached reasoning as a source of consolation in troubled times. "This philosophy which unfortunately depends much more on temperament than on reason"[16] is a frame of mind he must perforce adopt, contrary to his better judgment. Nostalgia to a great extent was forcing such moods upon him. "Man has only dreams and is himself only a dream,"[17] Maistre reflects in a particularly melancholy state of mind. Adèle, with whom he shared his views on literature, is the loved one to whom he addresses some somber, almost Romantic, reflections on life and the relentless passing of time: "My life flows by sadly. I watch the minutes which fall one after another into eternity; I count them, I assemble them, I make hours and days out of them, without ever experiencing even bitterness. At my age all illusions are ended; there remains only the family and that is what I miss. . . ."[18]

Affected by a profound sense of loss Maistre sought consolation in a stoical acceptance of his lot, but not without a very human emotional reaction to the hardships he faced. The homeland, with his friends and family, became a symbol of happier days. "Other hearts are strangers to me,"[19] is a typical utterance, providing an intimate revelation of the emptiness he experienced even when outwardly he gave the impression of adjusting easily to the Russian court.

When in the depths of despair, Maistre often expresses himself freely in the correspondence, thereby manifesting both his good and bad attitudes. Anti-Semitism, so regrettable in Voltaire and other *philosophes*, also infects the thinking of Maistre and results in some rather scurrilous comments on Jewish merchants in Saint-Petersburg. On the other hand, Maistre displays some powers of perception in observing that America has already reached a saturation point in colonization and that the future area of European expansion will be in Asia.

One of the more pleasant sides of Maistre's personality was still to be found in the casual and perceptive remarks made to Adèle on authors and literature. Alfieri, whose "ardent head" was almost totally spoiled by "modern philosophy," exemplified to the Count the ruinous effect of the Enlightenment on promising literary talent. Maistre implies he has read all of Alfieri's plays and advises Adèle to reevaluate her initial admiration of dramas like *Marie Stuart*: "No wise and informed judge will forgive Alfieri for having falsified history to satisfy the extravagance and stupid prejudice of the eighteenth century." Alfieri's connection with the Enlightenment, notwithstanding, there is no question in Maistre's mind that the dramatist was the "true creator of Italian tragedy."[20] The Count's appreciation of Alfieri's talent was to be shared by many young Romantics in the 1820s, among them, Lamartine.

While formulating his opinions of other writers Maistre's thoughts naturally focussed on his own literary efforts at the moment when the basic format of the *Soirées* was beginning to take shape in his mind: "For a long time . . . I have been turning over in my head certain dialogues on Providence, where I would show rather clearly, I think, that all these complaints bandied about on the impunity of crime are only ignorance and sophisms. . . ."[21]

More threatening in nature than the question of crime and punishment was the current situation in Europe, where the Allies suffered from a woeful lack of leadership by comparison with Napoleon and the French generals. From this dilemma Maistre sees a way out. A new order will be established in Europe so remarkable that it will provide a fit subject for a great work of literature: "Now I ask you whether among this host of captains and of statesmen who fight for our side, there are any one can put on an equal level with Napoleon and his band. . . . What is being prepared now in the world is one of the most marvelous spectacles that Providence has ever given to men, but the development of this plan is the subject of a book, not of a letter. . . ."[22]

The Revolution and Napoleon were inextricably bound to one another through the happenings that had rocked Europe; and they formed an unending theme in Maistre's writings. He repeats to one of Bonaparte's followers, Count d'Avaray, his contention that the material for an epic is to be found in the tragic events that took place in France. While speculating on future developments in literature the Count hints the time is ripe for a poetic renewal: "There is no longer any poetry in the world. . . . There is no longer any religion or love, but if it is ever reborn, the French Revolution will form the most noble subject of an epic poem. The long *errors* of your Master will form a rich episode of this poem. . . ."[23]

When envisaging the literature that would come out of the period dominated by Napoleon and the Revolution, Maistre had the Romantic's tendency to conceive of lofty designs fulfilled by leaders of heroic proportions. The secondrate hirelings he saw at the French Embassy in Saint-Petersburg around 1808 did not live up to his expectations. Even the enemy, he thought, should produce fine specimens of manhood. "The mediocrity of the persons by whom such big things are accomplished"[24] leaves a melancholy impression on Maistre. Despite his disillusionment he continues to harbor a desire to compose a literary work about the Napoleonic wars on a larger scale than the *Soirées*. It would remain for Hugo to accomplish this design.

The prospect of peace between France and Russia in 1808 compels

Maistre to entertain, in desperation, the wild dream of a personal interview with Napoleon. The Count, ordinarily inclined to be cautious and practical, feels that he is somehow capable of talking the Emperor into a favorable treaty with Sardinia: "If I could approach Napoleon, I would have ways of softening the lion."[25] Needless to say, his optimism did not last long.

Various aspects of Maistre's temperament and thinking become apparent throughout the correspondence. His odd position as the French-speaking ambassador of an Italian kingdom at the Russian court convinces him Providence has intervened in the life of one mortal, Joseph de Maistre; he sees himself plucked from obscurity in order to play a significant role at a critical period in the history of Europe: "Perhaps I was only good for the patriarchal life. . . . The Revolution ordained otherwise."[26] Now, faced with an arduous task, Maistre feels himself equal to the challenge. If he receives a snub from the Czar Maistre explains the oversight by a rather dry pun on his own name: "The Emperor *just about ignored me* . . . in the presence of masters *(maîtres)* he dare not be polite."[27]

The dilemma in Maistre's mind was the inability of men to judge when a significant historical event was good or bad for all concerned. Many kings attained power under questionable circumstances, although once on the throne the fact of their authority had to be accepted. One particular political reality long recognized in Europe was the rivalry between England and France — which Maistre explains by the power and prestige of both nations. He concludes that the peace of Europe depends ultimately on the reconciliation of these two powers. Lamartine, in 1848, as head of the provisional government, would have a similar view of the importance of peaceful relations between England and France. Most French Romantics for that matter were favorably disposed toward the English.

When not speculating dreamily on future developments in Europe Maistre could become quite sardonic. But, while he himself does not hesitate to give free rein to a satirical pen, Maistre excludes this very element from his definition of good comedy. "The joking and the ironical have nothing to do with the comical," he warns Adèle in 1809. "That is why Voltaire could never make a comedy; he makes lips laugh, but laughter from the heart, that which is called *good laughter*, can be experienced or aroused only by good people." Similarly, the Italian playwright Alfieri, although not deliberately malicious, is guilty of a certain innate harshness and bitterness that keeps him from attaining the level achieved by Molière in *L'Avare* and *Les Femmes savantes*. Alfieri, whom Maistre knew personally, took delight in writing a type of comedy which the Count labels *sarcasmodies*.[28] The explanation for this is the licentiousness revealed in Alfieri's memoirs, compared by Maistre to the shocking confessions of Rousseau. The Count's insistence on the moral factor as a yardstick for measuring a good writer brings to mind the moralism of Boileau and other Classical critics. As a result of an emphasis on the good and evil aspects of human conduct by Maistre, Baudelaire became concerned with the state of his moral life after reading the *Soirées*.

III *Maistre's Cultural Views*

Maistre's emphasis on the rigid intellectual formation necessary for writers explains his interest in the teaching of Latin and Greek. Upon learning of the decline of Latin studies in France, he unhesitatingly blames the educational theorists. Opening a book in Latin or Greek with the will to work hard was the only sound method in Maistre's experience: "It is rather amusing that those who do not know them wish absolutely to prove the evil of the methods employed by us who know them."[29]

A staunch conservative in matters pertaining to instruction, Maistre continued to be just as reactionary on the subject of feminine accomplishments. He probably was irritated by overly bright women in the salon, for that is precisely the impression he creates when denigrating the fair sex. No woman to his knowledge ever achieved lasting fame in the arts or sciences; and Maistre's advice to his daughter, Constance, would infuriate today's liberationists: "the woman's merit is in governing her house, making her husband happy, consoling him, encouraging him, raising his children, that is to say to *make men*."[30]

The prim and sober counsel given to Constance is echoed in the advice received by Adèle concerning great painters. Her father urges her to forget the superficial products of contemporaries and to concentrate instead on the outstanding artists of the not too distant past: "I imagine you do not wish to speak of the triumvirs of the great century, Lebrun, Lesueur, Poussin. Those three are worth more than many others. The third especially (in truth completely Italianized) is my hero; there is no painting that I understand better. As for the modern French artists, I leave them to you. . . ."[31]

Maistre's feeling of cultural superiority, as a Frenchman by training and tradition, generally caused him to regard French artists and writers as the European masters. With such a bias on questions of culture it is difficult for him to evaluate Russian civilization, which in his view is a direct result of the influence of the glittering but corrupt society of eighteenth-century France: "Their civilization, instead of developing gradually like ours, developed abruptly . . . circumstances put the Russian in contact with a nation which was at once the most active organ and the most deplorable victim of this corruption. . . ."[32]

If Maistre regrets the inroads of French rationalism in Russia he rather smugly observes the ease with which the French language asserts its superiority over its rivals in Saint-Petersburg. Italian, which the Czar deemed distasteful, was tolerated merely because of its use in the opera; otherwise French dominated the field.

IV *Maistre on Napoleon's Defeat*

With the termination of the short-lived alliance between France and Russia Maistre renewed his hopes for Sardinian independence. At the same time, rumors of an impending French invasion of Russia prompted Maistre to play the historical novelist and to size up almost intuitively the situation and the major protagonists in the coming struggle. Above all the Russian general, Kutusoff, intrigues Maistre. Unprepossessing in appearance, Kutusoff made his presence felt by his overpowering acumen: "Kutusoff is a man at least seventy years old, big and heavy, full of wit moreover, and exceedingly clever. . . . He is disfigured by a terrible wound; a bullet once pierced his head obliquely and went through the cavity of the eye. The globe is displaced and the other eye itself has suffered a good deal. . . ."[33] The prospect of the fate of Russia being placed in the hands of a doughty one-eyed marshal, not fully trusted by the Czar, must have presented to Maistre the format of a potentially powerful drama.

Once French armies were on Russian soil and the lack of thorough preparation by Bonaparte became evident, Maistre quickly predicted an imminent catastrophe:

Napoleon evidently is losing his head by advancing the way he does; he can no longer be saved, it seems to me, except by his star; but, when people entrust themselves to stars, in the end, they are duped. . . . Even when causing the trumpet to be sounded throughout Europe he suffers greatly and his disappointed hopes have thrown him in a state that borders sometimes on fury. . . .[34]

The contrast of the two leading figures, Kutusoff and Napoleon, lent an apocalyptic note to the unfolding drama; with grim amusement Maistre records the events he so long anticipated. After the carnage of the initial clashes of the two armies, the Count ponders somberly on war and battles: who is ultimately the victor?: "Very few battles are lost physically. . . . Battles are lost almost always morally; the real victor like the real loser is the one who believes he is. The battalions that advance, do they know they have fewer dead on their side? Those who retreat, do they know they have more [dead]? . . ."[35]

Although Maistre was quick to rejoice over any defeat of Bonaparte, he secretly deplored the cruelty and bloodshed of war, and when reflecting on the real implications of armed struggle between nations, was apt to draw rather bleak and morbid conclusions. Only his theory of reversibility could provide a logical explanation for the death of men in the prime of life. The innocent were atoning for the guilty, with the exception of the chief culprit, Napoleon, who was receiving his just deserts: "It is not an illusion at all; Bonaparte's star is fading."[36]

With harbingers of Napoleon's downfall Moscow became to Maistre the rallying point of Russian resistance against the tyrant. In the life of Russia the capital city was, in its unswerving loyalty to the Czar and in its deep religious faith, a symbol of the most profound traits of the nation. These qualities set Moscow apart from other European capitals. Consequently, the destruction of the city under French occupation united all Russians against the invaders: "For every nation . . . the capital is necessarily a sacred object surrounded by grand souvenirs, and a sort of crucible in which all the national ideas are fused together. . . . Moscow, in this category, surpassed perhaps all the other capitals. Political unity, religious unity, resided in its walls. . . ."[37]

The destruction of Moscow both appalled and fascinated Maistre, who sensed perhaps that the apocalyptic happenings he was inclined to predict were now upon him. Abandoning for a moment the usual precise and brisk style used in his correspondence, he waxes emotional and displays a pictorial imagination of the type later employed to good effect by Victor Hugo:

I would leave the style of narratives and assume that of poetry if I tried to describe the first five or six days. All the cellars caved in at the same time; an innumerable quantity of unchained and furious brigands; blood flowing in

the streets with wine and *eau-de-vie*; the two sides going at each others'
throats in the midst of the flames. . . . No language can render this spectacle
or even approach it. . . ."[38]

Maistre returns to his customary reserved and dignified irony
when commenting on the manner in which Napoleon started on the
road to defeat. While always convinced Bonaparte would eventually
fail he is nonetheless a bit startled by the rapid turn of events. One of
his favorite images is applied to depict Napoleon's dilemma, in
which the tyrant becomes his own executioner: "I never believed
one instant in the duration of the *monster* . . . but I did not think
at all his fall [was] so close. He had moreover the pleasure of
devouring himself, so the one suffering is just as noble as the
executioner. . . ."[39]

Once the defeat of Napoleon is assured Maistre writes more freely
on various topics, without feeling the pressure to put them aside in
order to pursue diplomatic questions relative to the status of Sardinia. Grateful to the English for their help in overthrowing
Napoleon, Maistre still bears a grudge against the nation that so
strongly influenced the Enlightenment in France. In a letter to one
of the foremost writers of the Catholic camp, the Vicomte de Bonald,
he fumes about the deleterious effect of the *philosophes*: "I would
like to return to our language the scepter of rational philosophy, but
the *beginning of wisdom* in philosophy is the scorn of English
ideas."[40]

V   *Maistre's Pre-Romanticism*

Sensitive to the beauties of the French Language — despite his
sallies against the *philosophes* — Maistre comments favorably on
Rousseau's talents as a stylist, so brilliantly exhibited in a celebrated
chapter in *Emile, La profession de foi du Vicaire Savoyard*: "The
most remarkable part of this work that has caused so much hubbub is
the *Profession of Faith of the Vicaire Savoyard;* the good and
bad it contains are found everywhere, but not in such beautiful
style. . . ."[41]

One noteworthy feature of Maistre's guarded praise of Rousseau is
the former's approval of the style of a chapter that came to be the
credo of Lamartine and other French Romantics. Too orthodox to
accept openly the sentimental deism of Rousseau, Maistre admits
nevertheless a favorable reaction to his adversary's artistry. The
Count's latent Romanticism was asserting itself; in spite of the
dogmatism that characterized many of Maistre's pronouncements on

theology, he remained aware of the irrational factors that played an important part in the spiritual life of many believers. Christianity had legends that bolstered the faith of its adherents; it mattered little to Maistre whether these tales were true. To be truly heartwarming religion must, he insists, appeal to the imagination as well as the intellect. Through the ages folklore in its legends transmitted many truths: "Behold Christian mythology! It is dramatic truth which has its value and its effect independently of literal truth . . . everyone is [a member of the] people on this point, and I know no one who is not impressed more by dramatic instruction than the fine maxims of moral philosophy and metaphysics."[42]

A further illustration of Maistre's acknowledgement that religion is not based entirely on intellectualization may be read in his remarks to Mme Swetechine, a prominent figure in continental social circles. Here Maistre is not at all the post-Tridentine theologian. Instead, he falls unknowingly into the category of those easy-going Catholic Romantics who perused with equal fervor the Bible and *Emile*. His emphasis on the intuition as the ultimate factor in conversion is, to say the least, uncharacteristic: "Conversion is a *sudden illumination.* . . . We have a great many examples of this kind, even in superior men [who are] the most capable of reasoning . . . the happy change is effected suddenly or by jolts; it always begins in the heart where the syllogism is a stranger. . . ."[43]

A tendency to adopt a Pascalian formula for conversion is traceable to the lingering influence of Saint-Martin, whose theosophy also stressed immediate access to the supernatural without the wearisome steps demanded by an overly systematic theology. Maistre remained loyal to Martinism, and, following the defeat of Napoleon, takes delight in relaxing and discussing in his letters the "disciples of Saint-Martin who are exalted Christians,"[44]

With the optimism acquired from his Martinist convictions — with their promise of divine guidance — Maistre entertained hope for the emergence of a spiritually rejuvenated Christianity: "All Europe is in a fermentation which is leading us to a religious revolution . . . for which the political revolution we have witnessed was only the frightful preface."[45] The preceding statement may suggest an even bloodier conflict over religion, but Maistre is thinking solely in terms of the far-reaching effects of a wholesale return to Catholicism, the only effective antidote to the poisonous doctrines of rationalism and Jacobinism: "If palingenesis is possible . . . it is only through the Church. The French Revolution is satanic; if the counterrevolution is not divine, it is nil. But where are the elements of this counterrevolution? . . ."[46]

Maistre proceeds to outline the dangers of the revolutionary ideas still found among partisans of Bonaparte and the Jacobins — in his opinion, ultimately identical. The count coyly hints that his writings may provide the necessary impetus for the desired counterrevolution, but he is too cautious to admit this openly. His solution for Europe's ills is not outlined in the form of finely detailed arguments, for Maistre entertains the theosophist's vision of a palingenesis, a radical transformation accomplished by replacing existing institutions with another system totally different in its religious and political philosophy. What Maistre foresees is a series of sweeping changes and a return to the spirit of medieval Europe. His prediction becomes that of a visionary, whose fancies and dreams overrule any sober and long-range planning. The Count assumes a more practical view of the situation only when contemplating the obstacles to a return to the heyday of the papacy. The mere thought of the *philosophes* is sufficient to remind him that an overnight reversal of the established order may not prove easy, since advocates of the Enlightenment have infiltrated all levels of society.

Closely linked to the Enlightenment was the Reformation created by German princes to rob the Church, according to Maistre's interpretation of history. These same forces, he confidently predicts, will be checked by the crowned heads of Europe to protect their own rights. "In the nineteenth (century) they will reestablish the Church in order to strengthen their thrones, put in jeopardy by Protestant principles."[47]

Maustre was consistent in his belief that a return to the old order was imperative if religious and political sanity were to be preserved in the years to come. The theory of progress was totally rejected and supplanted in Maistre's thinking by the notion that a step backward in time was a salutary thing. "The grand pretention of our age is to believe itself very superior to all the others; and the fact is however that it is very inferior; it is always in contradiction with ancient common sense."[48]

Proof to support this statement was easy for Maistre to adduce. Revolutionary ferment had not ceased in Europe with the defeat of Napoleon. Jacobins were reappearing in France and subversive forces were at work elsewhere in Europe. "If the revolutionary party gets out of this safe and sound," he warns, "without having lost all the fruit of the Revolution, the cause of Sovereignty is lost."[49]

In the face of these ominous forces Maistre continues to seek solace in a dream of a millenium in which the powers of evil will be miraculously overcome. His apocalyptic vision is vividly described to the Czar's minister, Prince Korlowski:

A thousand reasons, too long to elaborate, prove to me we are touching on a moral and religious revolution, without which chaos will never give way to creation. The hand of Providence is making itself felt visibly . . . we still see nothing, because up to now it has only cleaned the place; but our children will cry out with respectful admiration: *He who is powerful accomplished great things for us. . . .*"[50]

Later in the century, during the full tide of Romanticism, Maistre would have been more at home with his imaginative concepts of a millenium and the reestablishment of an ideal order, after the expiation demanded by God as the *sine qua non*. Living in a transitional period he combines in his personality and outlook the defensiveness of a Catholic absolutist, the mordant irony of a confirmed Voltairean, and the transcendental theosophy of a Martinist. What results from this combination is at times perplexing. Maistre is alternately dogmatic, skeptical, and mystical. As formidable as these traits might appear, they represented only one side of a man who like most humans experienced the pains of frustration and loneliness. His stay in Russia after Waterloo was now coming to an end. Plagued by a shortage of funds he bitterly described the solitude imposed by a prolonged separation from his family: "Woe to the man born in a separate land who goes to establish himself in the dominant country, where he has neither status, family, nor property. He will never take root there; he will only be *put* there, as a plate is *put* on a table to be used a moment and then taken away after having been soiled. . . ."[51]

The extent of Maistre's actual isolation in Russia is revealed in his own admission that he did not speak Russian even after a long residence in Saint-Petersburg: "I know . . . only the single word, *khorocho*, indispensable at each moment to praise everything that is done."[52] Maistre's sense of emptiness in leaving his loved ones behind undoubtedly explains this failure to learn Russian by a person with a natural flair for languages. Prepared at any moment to be recalled by his king he saw no need to study a difficult tongue. Besides, French was the fashionable language at Court and Maistre was too involved with writing his own work — when not conversing with émigrés from Sardinia and France on the prospects of the restoration of rightful rulers to their thrones.

Toward the end of his stay in Russia Maistre, reassessing his accomplishments, apparently concludes the results are too indefinite for an adequate evaluation. The person who works silently, he muses, may do more in the end with little fanfare: "I prostrate myself before the one . . . who could instruct, console, relieve his fellowmen . . . these heroes of silent charity who hide themselves and expect nothing in this world."[53]

VI   *Return to Savoy and Last Period*

Maistre's last months at Saint-Petersburg were brightened by the arrival of his family. Following this reunion, his thoughts turned increasingly to his native Savoy. Having at last arranged his passage on a Russian man-of-war bound for France, he displays in his final letters written in Russia little sorrow in leaving the place of exile. Uppermost in his mind, judging from his correspondence with Louis de Bonald, is the publication of his literary works. The favor of the Vicomte de Bonald, who survived the Bonaparte regime to be highly regarded by Louis XVIII, would be a strong factor in assuring Maistre a place in the literary world. Recognition for the Count was already partly guaranteed by the works published before and during his sojourn in Saint-Petersburg.

Once back in Turin he followed with interest the fortunes of Louis XVIII and the Bourbon restoration. Much more hopeful now — in an era when legitimately crowned heads occupied Europe's thrones — Maistre contemplates the possibility of sudden unforeseen developments, despite the threat of further violence in France: "The evil is such that it evidently announces a divine explosion."[54] His prophecy of the imminence of an apocalyptic era of far-reaching theological importance is repeated to Bonald with the reminder that in the *Soirées*, "I gathered all the signs (I mean those to my knowledge) which announce some great event in the religious circle."[55] Unquestionably the *Soirées*, to which Maistre was referring, was the work closest to his heart, the one containing his philosophical and mystical analysis of Europe's future.

The final pages of the correspondence see a renewal of the assault on Condillac and the ideologues and a restatement of Maistre's belief in the divine origin of language: "One has to be possessed by four or five devils to believe in the invention of language."[56]

By the same token Mme de Staël's pronouncements on the French Revolution are dismissed by Maistre as the ravings of an impertinent little woman who does not understand one of the questions she treats.[57] Without altering his opinions, Maistre, somewhat later, heartily indorses Bonald's criticism of Mme de Staël's *Considérations sur la Révolution francaise:* "I do not know whether I would have been as kind, for very few books exasperate me as much as those of Mme de Staël. . . . What a shame this woman was not a spiritual subject of legitimate sovereignty! . . ."[58] Maistre's wish that Mme de Staël would embrace Catholicism was born of a desire to see her intellectual gifts put to better use. Religious considerations did not let him lose sight of her genius. In fact, to his credit, the Count did not judge any writer superior who happened to be a Catholic; his reservations concerning a noted contemporary obliged him to caution a youthful correspondent: "You say that the Eternal created *Chateaubriand to guide the universe.* One sees well, excellent young man, you are eighteen."[59]

Little analysis is required to deduce Maistre's probable opinion of Chateaubriand and of the *Génie du Christianisme,* with its Rousseauistic interpretation of Catholic beliefs and liturgy. Most likely Maistre refrained from an outright attack on Chateaubriand through a desire not to undermine an author who had in some manner counteracted the Enlightenment. Concern with seeing his manuscripts in print would also impel Maistre to speak discreetly of an author who might intercede on his behalf with a prospective publisher.

Maistre's link with the rising generation of Romantics was established through his contacts with Lamennais and Lamartine. The former, author of the *Essai sur l'Indifférence,* held many views in common with Maistre. Together with Bonald they espoused the principles of Traditionalism, the Catholic school of thought that traced language and the fundamental principles of knowledge to an immediate gift from God. This group came to be known as the Theocrats. Though more liberal in orientation, Lamartine was not unaffected by Traditionalism, owing to his friendship with Lamennais and Maistre. "You have founded an unperishable school of high philosophy and Christian politics,"[60] the poet of the *Méditations* informed Maistre in 1820. Although he would later abandon a strictly Catholic and royalist position, Lamartine was perhaps more deeply affected by his acquaintance with Maistre than he cared to admit. Like the Count, Lamartine was inclined to be mystical; he believed in an order not readily apparent to the senses and beyond the scope of ordinary human knowledge.

A perusal of the correspondence discloses a multifaceted Joseph de

Maistre. Diplomat and political philosopher, he was also a loving father, a warmhearted friend, and a keen student of literature. Rigorously dogmatic when speaking as a Catholic apologist, he had a deeply mystical temperament. The current crisis in Europe foreshadowed a new order, after the proper expiation had been made and man's spirit regenerated; such was the vision of the devout Martinist.

While admiring the talent of illustrious contemporaries Maistre stated forthrightly his disagreement with their views. Mme de Staël is sternly, but not unjustly, criticized, and appropriate recognition is made of her literary powers. There is evidence of a slight disapproval of Chateaubriand but no outright attack on a writer with whom he shared not a few ideas in common. Cordial letters from Lamartine and Lamennais indicate that Maistre had words of encouragement for aspiring young writers.

Maistre's literary views expressed in the correspondence reveal a writer of both Classical and Romantic tendencies. A staunch supporter of Corneille, Racine, and Molière, he preferred nonetheless a dramatic theory that encouraged more spontaneity in manner and a natural tone of voice. He was uncompromisingly moralistic in his demands for purity in literature and yet surprisingly sensitive to the delicacy of Rousseau's style. The extent of his innate Romanticism is discernible not only in his stylistic preferences but in his recognition that human motivation is often explainable by motives that spring from the heart rather than by ideas calmly analyzed by an objective intellect.

A final word might be added on Maistre's perception of history in terms of majestic events and of the men who played significant roles in them. Regardless of his praise or criticism of the individuals involved, Maistre invariably judged most of them, including a nemesis like Napoleon, as instruments in God's plans to institute a new order. If Maistre had not been hampered by diplomatic duties he might well have turned to the historical novel, a genre for which he was well suited by reason of his literary talents, interpretations of history, and imaginative faculties.

CHAPTER 7

Maistre's Literary Fortunes in France

I Critical Reaction in the Nineteenth Century

L ITTLE imagination is required to picture the reaction of the *philosophes* had Maistre been one of their contemporaries. The presence of a Catholic writer capable of matching wits with Voltaire would not have been taken lightly; there would be a steady stream of satirical writings in reply to the diatribes of a sharp-tongued critic of the Enlightenment. Rousseau would tremble with rage at the Sardinian upstart's attacks on *Emile* and the *Social Contract*.

As things turned out Maistre's career began three decades after the death of the leading *philosophes*. His two illustrious contemporaries, Mme de Staël and Chateaubriand, while differing with him on many points, at least espoused some form of Christianity. Chateaubriand seems to have sensed Maistre's disapproval of him when declining gracefully to become involved in the publication of *Du Pape*. As a result of his friendly disputes with Mme de Staël in Switzerland the latter could harbor no illusions about the extent of their disagreement on numerous issues. Still, she remarked after meeting Maistre in Saint-Petersburg in 1812, "A Russian desire, said a superior man, would make a city jump."[1] Her encounters with Maistre probably always ended in a battle of wits. Maistre obviously enjoyed her company and, when Mme de Staël was on her deathbed, sought in vain through the intercession of Mme Swetchine to see his friendly adversary in Paris.

Even warmer ties were established with other contemporaries. Bonald and Lamennais welcomed him into the Catholic camp that expected great things of the Restoration. Royalist periodicals lavished praise on Maistre as a leading spokesman for rightful authority and religion.

In analyzing the period in which Maistre wrote, Sainte-Beuve ranked him with Mme de Staël and Chateaubriand: "Three writers of the greatest renown made their début . . . at the same moment . . . under the exciting impulse of the French Revolution."[2] The *Considérations sur la France* intrigued Sainte-Beuve with its "prophetic audacity"[3] and represented to the critic the very cornerstone on which Maistre subsequently based other works. Penetrating the maze of political arguments and metaphysical subtleties in Maistre's work, Sainte-Beuve marvels at both the Classical purity of his style and the Romantic elements born of a clairvoyant imagination. There was no doubt in Sainte-Beuve's mind that Maistre's work would endure. One book, in particular, assured the writer posthumous fame: "The *Soirées* is the finest work by M. de Maistre, the most durable, the one that addresses itself to the most numerous class of free and intelligent readers. . . . In his work imagination and color in the bosom of a lofty thought make eternal problems ever present. . . ."[4]

Sainte-Beuve wondered how an author, presumably a strict Catholic, could dabble to such an extent in the occult and envision a future in which many religious, political, and social changes would take place. An inflexibly orthodox and dogmatic person would ordinarily have no room in his scheme of things for any dynamic principles admitting the possibility of a millenium in which old values would give way to a new order. This aspect of Maistre's thinking must have attracted Lamartine, who seems in so many ways diametrically opposed to the Count. Actually, apart from the degree of each writer's adherence to Catholic teaching, they were not too far apart in their overall view of religion and philosophy. Even then Maistre judged Catholicism no obstacle to the study of Martinism and theosophic speculations on the future of European civilization. Elements in Lamartine's eclecticism parallel, in what is more than sheer coincidence, some essential features of Maistre's outlook presented in the *Soirées*. Hinduism, Saint-Martin, and a universal cult uniting all religions and points of view were accepted more or less by both Lamartine and Maistre.[5] In the twilight of his own career in the 1850s the poet reminisced at length about Maistre in the *Cours familier de litterature*. Irked by the Count's dogmatism Lamartine minced no words in berating the tirades against heresy in *Du Pape*. A more gentle and sympathetic tone was adopted in recalling personal contacts with Maistre. To Lamartine's credit he gave a balanced criticism of Maistre and displayed appreciation of the Sardinian's verve and originality. The *Soirées*, in particular, evoked

Lamartine's praise and criticism, as the poet lauded the work's fine style and decried its shortcomings: "Such is this book . . . a style astonishing in its vigor and flexibility, new, profound insights immeasurable in their range concerning legislation, dogmas, mysteries, and sometimes pleasantries out of place in serious subject matter . . . a declamatory Diderot in a sincere and Christian philosopher. . . ."[6]

Whereas Lamartine was struck by the mystical and prophetic insights of Joseph de Maistre, Alfred de Vigny was at once fascinated and horrified by the concept of reversibility stressed so dreadfully in the *Soirées*. Doctor Noir, in *Stello*, castigates Joseph de Maistre and the abominable concepts of the innocent atoning for the guilty and of war as an instrument of divine justice. Maistre is denounced as a monstrous charlatan: "It was necessary for this pitiless sophist to blow, like a patient alchemist, on the dust of the first books, on the ashes of the first doctors, on the powder of the Indian *bûchers* [funeral pyres], and cannibalistic feasts to make the incendiary spark of the fatal idea come forth. . . ."[7] Despite Vigny's aversion to Maistrean doctrines on expiation and regeneration, he apparently could not forget entirely the vivid portrait of the inevitability of human suffering in the *Soirées*. More than one poem by Vigny seems affected in part by Maistrean imagery. Does not Moses in a sense bear the burden of his people's indifference? As for Christ in the *Mont des Oliviers*, what better example of Maistre's principle of reversibility could be found? In short, Vigny's basic contention that the superior man must endure the hardships imposed by a cruel Fate is strongly Maistrean in its underlying rationale.

Of the other leading Romantic poets, Hugo and Musset had no direct connection with Maistre. However, in view of Sainte-Beuve's mention of the Count as one of the three precursors of French Romanticism, the general influence of the *Soirées* can not be entirely disregarded. Musset's complaints about the lack of a firm religious orientation that plagued him throughout his life may be partly attributable to a perception of Maistrean Catholicism as an ideal that promised certitude at the price of individual freedom. To one of Musset's individualism the cost was high indeed. In contrast to Musset Hugo's customary optimism could not countenance the pessimism of Maistre. Still, both Hugo and Maistre investigated the same general sources of theosophy, Saint-Martin, Swedenborg, and their followers. For this reason the similarity between Hugo's belief in both an invisible world and an eventual millenium and Maistre's beliefs is not at all coincidental.

Stendhal of course was not attracted by Maistre's theosophy — which to the caustic rationalist was tantamount to primitive mumbo-jumbo. In his articles written for English journals Stendhal denounced the absurdity of Maistre's political philosophy and his inordinate emphasis on papal authority. The arrogance of the Jesuits and the fanaticism of young French priests were imputable, Stendhal maintained, in no small part to the bigoted writings of the Count: "Priests are young peasants, all more or less imbued, unfortunately, with a spirit of fanaticism. They come from seminaries established by the Jesuits, in which they are taught the doctrines of the famous M. de Maistre, a writer who may, at this moment, be regarded as the French St. Paul. . . ."[8] Stendhal's dislike of Maistre unquestionably stiffened his anticlerical opposition to the Jesuits and the Church. His attitude was characteristic of many French writers in the nineteenth century, for whom the Count epitomized the worst features of uncompromising dogmatism.

Balzac, in the *Mémoires de Sanson*, employs familiar Maistrean imagery to summarize the effects of the upheaval precipitated by the fall of the Bastille: "The Revolution has passed and from the depths to which it descended there has not come forth a great [period of] meditation. The most widespread abuse has not been sufficient to demonstrate the atrocity of custom; the death sentence has not been abolished . . . the law still demands human sacrifices. . . ."[9] Opposed to Maistre's teaching on the role of the executioner Balzac, like Vigny, rejects the doctrine of reversibility and all it entails. On the subject of monarchy and the divine right of kings Balzac's viewpoint is more compatible with that of Joseph de Maistre. In addition, he agreed in general with Maistre on the existence of a primitive revelation and on the divine origin of language.

Among writers of a literary school other than Balzacian Realism, Nodier and Nerval were by nature favorably disposed to certain aspects of Maistre's writing and philosophy. Nodier was acquainted with Saint-Martin and in his *Contes* displayed a deep awareness of an invisible and intangible world closely connected with the prosaic world of reality; Michel, in the *Fée aux miettes*, is a fairly close approximation of Maistre's innocent victim who suffers vicariously for the sins of others. Michel also must submit to a period of regeneration and is instructed by the *Fée aux miettes* in occult sciences that originated in Chaldaea, an idea considered in the *Soirées*. Nerval also traced the origin of religion to Chaldean sources and had the same general view as Maistre on crime and punishment. Like

Maistre, Nodier and Nerval had considerable contact with Freemasonry and its symbolism. Theosophic principles traceable partly to Saint-Martin form a substantial part of Nerval's theories of the subconscious; Nerval might well have been introduced to the "unknown philosopher" through a reading of the *Soirées.*

Acquaintance with Maistre and acceptance of his teachings on religion and politics are discernible in the most unlikely quarters. The Count's appeal to Nodier and Nerval is understandable but few would expect the positivist, Auguste Comte, to be his enthusiastic disciple. But Comte, surprisingly, encountered in Maistre a man after his own mind. In *Du Pape,* the *Soirées,* and the *Considérations,* the father of positivism read a justification of the absolute necessity of a moral order and a detailed, logical description of primitive society. Even more surprising is the fact that Comte was introduced to Maistre by Saint-Simon, who found in the *Soirées* and in the *Considérations* the outlines of a society based on morality and free from revolutionary chaos. Needless to say Comte and Saint-Simon eliminated the Catholicism inherent in Maistre's theories.[10]

Pierre Ballanche, who had much in common with Maistre as a theosophist anticipating society's expiation and generation, considered the Count too old-fashioned for modern times: "the man of ancient doctrines, the prophet of the past . . . and whom one would like in vain to resuscitate."[11]

A French Protestant, Edmond Schérer, could be expected to take exception to Maistre's attacks against the Reformation. By the middle of the nineteenth century Schérer judged Maistre too outmoded to be given serious consideration and tried to imagine what the Count might say if he returned to visit France in the 1850s: "What would he say . . . in noticing that the center of gravity in the world has moved and that modern civilization is essentially a Protestant civilization?"[12]

To a thinker like Renan, the antithesis in almost every respect of Joseph de Maistre, the Count was an idiosyncratic dogmatist who rushed to conclusions for the sake of justifying any conceivable thesis: ". . . Joseph de Maistre, a great lord impatient with the slow discussions of philosophy. For God's sake! a decision and let it be ended, true or false, little matter. The important thing is that I be at rest. . . ."[13]

Faguet also was perplexed by the mercurial disposition of Maistre, a defect that made the polemicist's tirades susceptible of several interpretations. Maistre was alternately Catholic and atheist to Faguet, who was at a loss to analyze him thoroughly: "Very often in reading the *Soirées* one thinks he is reading *Candide*. . . . One can read two to three hundred pages of him and take him for an atheist. . . . I remain astonished before this Christianity where I do not find Christ himself. . . . Jesus for him is a 'bloody victim' and nothing more. . . ."[14]

II *Maistre in the Twentieth Century*

The era prior to World War I witnessed a substantial Maistre revival. Neomonarchism flourished and a renewal in Catholicism affected the thinking of artists and writers. Jacques Maritain, the neo-scholastic, marked a return to the orthodox and disciplined metaphysics of Thomas Aquinas. Many writers of divergent backgrounds and dispositions, among them Charles Péguy and Paul Bourget, were reexamining the Church. A typical product of this reemphasis on Catholicism was Ernest Psichari, a young writer who, like Péguy and other members of that literary generation, died in combat with the Germans.

In *L'Appel des armes* Psichari recounts his military service in North Africa through the central character, Captain Timothée Nangès. A sensual fellow given to a voluptuous life style with a mistress and other worldly comforts, Nangès, nonetheless, cherishes the Church and the military, the two foundations of the French nation. Unconcerned about original sin Nangès questions in Maistrean fashion the value of the theory of progress. Psichari encountered similar problems shortly before his conversion to Catholicism in 1913. Like other writers, among them Péguy and Barrès, Psichari was struck by the theological antitheses and symbolism in Pascal and Maistre; the religious experience growing out of the challenge to Psichari posed by the two writers is recorded in *L'Appel des armes* in Nangès' quandary: "What he needed then was a Catholic thought. . . . He went to Pascal or Joseph de Maistre. Quite naturally, he turned to these fine erect stems, without adventitious branches or *protrusions* and from which all the *sap* is hurled toward the sky, gushes forth vertically from the earth to the zenith. . . ."[15]

The fiery Léon Bloy, in a journal conserving his impressions of the 1890s, stressed France's unique position as a nation essential to the fulfillment of God's plans for Europe. Bloy, by his own admission, restated an earlier prognostication by Maistre: "France is not another nation like the others. It is the only one *which God needs*, Maistre said, who was sometimes a prophet. There will always be in her, whatever is done, a principle of sovereign life, which nothing could destroy."[16]

Whether or not a nationalistic interpretation of French Catholicism was irreconcilable with Church teaching mattered little to Bloy. In many ways Bloy was a neo-Romantic, rejecting the documentation of Catholic theologians to create his own mystic, intuitive, and somewhat arbitrary interpretation of history. To Bloy, a latterday Joseph de Maistre, historical symbolism transcended in significance the full factual approach of presumably scientific historians. In Bloy's perspective of history a clement Providence guided not only man in general but also the destiny of nations, a distinctly Maistrean view of society and world order.

Bourget, another writer with a highly individualistic concept of French Catholicism and nationalism, wrote in *Pages de critique et de doctrine* about one of Maistre's close friends, the Marquis Costa de Beauregard. In a short essay Bourget refers to "a striking description" in the *Soirées* of a trip on the Po River from Turin to Venice.[17]

Maistre was then widely read, especially by Catholics, during the resurgence of interest in the Church in the period before, during, and immediately following World War I. Marshal Foch's concept of the power of moral forces in history seemed to parallel that of Maistre. Charles Maurras, a political thinker of neomonarchist leanings, found much in Maistre to admire and pointed out quite justifiably the extent to which the Count's philosophy had been distorted and misrepresented:[18] "This upright spirit, who, seeing with a pitiless lucidity the saddest, the harshest laws of life, made it his duty to admit what he saw just as he saw it, was not hard-hearted. . . . He left ferocity, even harshness, to the idyllic *massacrers* of the Revolution, the Saint-Justs and the Robespièrres. . . ."[19]

Later, in the twentieth century, interest in Maistre continued unabated. Camus, in *L'Homme revolté*, drew a parallel between Maistre and Karl Marx. Both men, as political thinkers, were inclined to be fatalists, and though they operated on widely different premises there were definite similarities in their approach to the establishment of a new order:

We find in Marx the same sort of creative fatalism. Maistre undoubtedly justified the established order. But Marx justifies the order which is established in his time. . . . Another order must be established which will demand, in the name of history, a new conformity. As for the means, they are the same for Marx as for Maistre: political realism, discipline, force. . . .[20]

With the centenary of Maistre's death in 1921 scholars were once more moved to reevaluate his works. In the period during World War II there was evidence of the perennial appeal of the Count's work to philosophers and writers, who, in a study of France's past, found problems and solutions applicable in no small measure to the twentieth century. Despite Maistre's absolutist approach to political questions his verve and originality could still catch the fancy of a new generation. Bernard de Vaulx became excited about Maistre's inventive approach to politics, and Baron Michaud outlined to readers how the Count had answers to the contemporary anguish in France. To Stanislas Fumet the *Principe générateur* even by modern standards remained a masterpiece of penetration.[21] Researchers, bent on exploring the current of irrationalism in the eighteenth century and its effect on Romanticism, eagerly reexamined the writings of Maistre.

Today less attention is paid to the Count's theological extremism. Emphasis on an ecumenical view of religious differences has removed the acrimony arising from past disputes. Protestants, freethinkers, and Catholics are inclined on the whole to analyze Maistre impartially as an arresting figure in political science, philosophy, and literature; they are willing to ignore his role as an inflexible polemicist.

As a parting thought it might be observed that Maistrean ideology has by no means lost its relevance to French politics. The late Charles de Gaulle embodied, in many respects, many principles which the irrepressible Count would heartily approve. In some ways General de Gaulle may be regarded as the embodiment of the Chevalier of the *Soirées*.

III   *Maistre and Baudelaire*

The extent of Maistre's influence on Baudelaire has been already treated by a number of critics.[22] Catholicism, it is generally agreed, constituted a significant part of Baudelaire's heritage and Maistre, more than any other writer, deeply affected the Catholic phases of the poet's thinking. Unconcerned about the Church in his youth, Baudelaire, when troubled by religious, social and political questions later in life, turned to Maistre for an interpretation of Catholicism. Certain attitudes in Baudelaire are strongly tinged with Maistrean ideas.

Baudelaire was receptive to Maistre after his disillusionment with the failure of the revolution of 1848 and the subsequent *coup d'état* by Louis-Napoléon in 1851. Bitterly disappointed by the shortlived dream of social utopias and democracy, Baudelaire found the antidote for his frustration in Maistre's austere authoritarian formula for the regeneration of society. The Count's aristocratic political ideas and pessimistic view of mankind made a lasting impression on Baudelaire, who may have been introduced to Maistre upon reading Vigny's comments in *Stello*. In complete disagreement with Vigny's criticism of Maistre, Baudelaire has nothing but praise for the author of the *Soirées*.

In his biography of Poe, Baudelaire used Maistre's curt condemnation of Locke's bourgeois commercialism, "What a stench of the market-place!"[23] to excoriate the materialism of middle class values. Many other references to Maistre are to be found in Baudelaire's writing, all of which concern various phases of the Count's religious and philosophical outlook. There is no evidence that Baudelaire was interested in the details of Maistre's life.

Unlike the mainstream of Romanticism, which accepted on the whole the Rousseauistic dream of man's natural goodness, unthwarted by the cruel restrictions imposed by the laws of an unjust society, Baudelaire was unsatisfied with this optimistic explanation of human nature. Instead, the poet became convinced that restlessness and unhealthy appetites in man stemmed from other causes. In a letter to a friend in 1856 Baudelaire asks: "Just what is the naturally good man? . . . The naturally good man would be a *monster*. . . . All the heresies to which I alluded just now are after all only the consequence of the great modern heresy . . . I mean, the suppression of the idea of *original sin*."[24] Even in one of his prose poems, "Le gateau," Baudelaire sees the fist fight between two regamuffins over a piece of cake as a proof of original sin and a refutation of the theory of natural goodness.

If original sin, so graphically depicted in the *Soirées*, is a guiding principle in much of human conduct, then it follows logically in Baudelaire's mind that the eighteenth-century theory of progress is equally invalid. Once more Maistre's denunciations of the Enlightenment are echoed by Baudelaire: "What is more absurd than Progress? . . . Progress will have atrophied so thoroughly in us all the spiritual part, that nothing, among the sanguinary, sacrilegious, or antinatural reveries of the utopians, will be able to be compared to its positive results.[25]

So lasting was the impression made on Baudelaire by Maistre's insistence on the reign of evil in the world that the poet may have been moved by the haunting descriptions of wickedness in the *Soirées* to entitle his celebrated work *Les Fleurs du mal*. To Baudelaire evil was a recurrent theme inevitably treated in poetry: "Since the beginning of poetry, all the volumes of poetry are composed thus. But it was impossible to do otherwise a book designed to represent *the agitation of the spirit in evil.* . . ."[26]

Although during his rebellious youth Baudelaire sang boldly the praises of Satan, he eventually accepted more and more Maistre's arguments on the power of evil. George Sand's blithe acceptance of the Rousseauistic notion of natural goodness incited the poet to denounce her theories with an orthodox vigor reminiscent of Maistre: "The abolishers of souls *(materialists)* are necessarily abolishers of hell; they certainly have a *self-interest.* . . . Sand is for the *God of good people.* . . . *The Devil and George Sand.* . . ."[27] The sentimental novelist was not alone in exercising a baleful influence on the minds of man. The attitude and thought of Voltaire, a carry-over from the Enlightenment, infected all too many segments of French life and culture. In a mood characteristic of Maistre Baudelaire sighs regretfully, "I grow weary in France, especially when everyone here resembles Voltaire." Baudelaire in fact goes as far as Maistre in tracing Voltaire's lack of the poetic spirit to a denial of the soul's immortality: "Voltaire jokes about this immortal soul."[28]

While Maistre led Baudelaire away from the theories of the Enlightenment and back to a more Catholic view of religion and philosophy, he also exercised a positive influence in molding the poet's views on prayer and meditation: "Prayer is a reservoir of strength. . . . There is in prayer a magical operation. Prayer is one of the greatest forces of the intellectual dynamic. There is there something like an electrical recurrence. . . ."[29]

Closely connected to a belief in prayer, as outlined by Maistre, was an acceptance of the Count's theory of reversibility. The title of one of Baudelaire's poems, "Réversibilité," hints at a direct borrowing, while the poet's arguments against capital punishment are unmistakably colored by Maistre's reasoning on the same general subject: "The death penalty is the result of a mystic idea totally uncomprehended today. The death penalty, materially at least, does not have as its end *saving* society. It has as its end to save [spiritually] society and the guilty person. In order for the sacrifice to be perfect, there must be assent and joy on the part of the victim."[30]

In an area other than theology Maistre's ideas had a strong effect on Baudelaire. Disgusted with democracy, the poet had little difficulty accepting the Count's arguments in favor of an aristocracy, since it was obvious to Baudelaire that in a republic artists were out of style. While not interested in the fine points of Maistre's speculations on political science Baudelaire favored the general outlines of an aristocratic system in which creative genius would be recognized. The poet's frequently expressed preference for the stability of aristocratic rule leaves little doubt about his distaste for popular rule. Political upheaval of any kind was repugnant to Baudelaire: "There is in every change something at once infamous and agreeable, something which stems from infidelity and removal. That suffices to explain the French Revolution."[31] Maistre's objections to the policy of Bonaparte recall similar criticism by Baudelaire of the Second Empire under the first Emperor's nephew, Louis-Napoléon.

Maistre's reflections on the harmony maintained by the power of Providence throughout the universe may have had some effect on Baudelaire's concept of the correspondences perceived everywhere by the poet. Much of this of course is traceable to Hoffman, Lavater, Fourier, and Swedenborg. Still, in view of Baudelaire's respect for Maistre, the latter cannot be ruled out altogether in any analysis of the poet's aesthetics. A well-known passage from the "Correspondances" has a perceptibly Maistrean flavor: "Nature is a temple where living pillars allow at times confused words to issue forth; man passes through forests of symbols which observe him with familiar glances."[32] In the above quotation there is a touch of the theosophic, in keeping with Maistre's espousal of Saint-Martin. Both Baudelaire, in the "Correspondances," and the Count, in the *Soirées*, termed nature a temple. From the *Soirées* Baudelaire may have acquired as well a conception of the harmony and order of the universe.

Sartre's thought-provoking study of Baudelaire provides many useful insights to the student but oversimplifies the question of Maistre's relationship to Baudelaire. The eminent existentialist apparently allows a latent feeling of hostility toward Catholicism to blur his perception of Baudelaire's debt to the Count. Feelings about the Church in Baudelaire's time differed greatly from the atmosphere of disillusionment in which existentialism thrived after World War II. Lamartine and Vigny were returned to the fold upon their death in the 1860s when signs of the Catholic Revival were already beginning to appear. Unlike the sentimental *renouveau* initiated by Chateaubriand earlier in the century, the later resurgence of Catholicism was marked by a stronger emphasis on orthodoxy.

Baudelaire's obsession with original sin was indicative in some measure of a rebirth of interest in Catholic theology among certain intellectuals.

The reaction of any creative writer, especially one of Baudelaire's temperament, to a particular school of philosophy or religion must of course be evaluated rather cautiously. But given Baudelaire's enthusiasm for Maistre, expressed so frequently in correspondence and miscellaneous writings, any effort to minimize the Count's influence is necessarily made on very tenuous grounds. From that standpoint it is reasonable to assume Baudelaire's Catholicism was Maistrean if not Roman.

The effect of Maistre's writings on Baudelaire substantiates Sainte-Beuve's conclusion that Maistre ranked with Chateaubriand and Madame de Staël as one of the leading precursors of Romanticism. If the period in which Baudelaire wrote is accepted as the last phase of Romanticism—a view held by the poet—Maistre's overall influence on the Romantic movement becomes increasingly significant. The Count himself little suspected that his work would affect a broad spectrum of French writers of diverse dispositions and aesthetic outlooks.

would remain a constant threat. The frightening symbolism of the soldier and the executioner, grimly fulfilling their respective roles on the battlefield and in civilian life, made an enduring impression on many readers, some of whom became important writers in their own right.

Central to Maistre's program for the rejuvenation of a Catholic monarchist Europe was the reestablishment of France as the continent's leader, a mission for which the French nation was preordained by divine will. With some qualifications writers over a century later were to reemphasize the Maistrean dream of French hegemony. Neomonarchism in the twentieth century represented in no small degree a restatement of the Count's message in the *Soirées*.

Sainte-Beuve's conclusion that Maistre ranked with Chateaubriand and Mme de Staël as a precursor of Romanticism is unhappily overlooked today in the usual assessment of literary developments in nineteenth-century France. In several respects Maistre, more than his two contemporaries, incorporated in theory and practice both Classical and Romantic views. The clarity, wit, and style of Classicism were combined with the color and imagination of Romanticism. To this combination Maistre brought his own peculiar insights born of Catholic orthodoxy and theosophic mysticism. While resulting at times in undue fanaticism, Maistre's genius nonetheless enriched a period which, with few exceptions, suffered from the usual artistic stagnation of an era of transition. His name today deserves a better fate than a routine assignment to the list of secondary influences on Romanticism. Joseph de Maistre is in need not only of reevaluation but rediscovery.

Notes and References

Chapter One

1. For biographical details readers are referred to works listed in the section on bibliography.
2. See *The Writings of Mme Swetchine*, ed. F. A. P. de Falloux, trans. H. Preston (Boston, 1869).
3. The *Éloge de Victor-Amédée* and the *Discours sur la vertu* are not available in a complete text. Excerpts were published in the following work: F. Descostes, *Joseph de Maistre avant la Révolution* (Paris, 1893), I, 289 - 312; II, 38 - 50.
4. Ibid., I, 290, 291. Unless otherwise noted all translations are my own. The French text is given for complete sentences and long phrases but not for brief phrases or expressions. "La louange est un crime quand on la prostitue au vice. . . . /L'ambition, l'intérêt, l'orgueil, la volupté, tous les vices se présentent sur les marches du trône. . . ."
5. Ibid., I, 292, 293. "Je tremble quand je vois les liens de la société commencent à se relâcher parmi nous./. . . *Qui ne commencent à réfléchir que quand le cri des peuples leur annonce que tout est perdu.* . . ."
6. Ibid., I, 295. "C'est elle qui lui apprend que ses sujets sont *ses frères;* c'est elle qui lui montre, au dela du trépas, un juge formidable qui jettera dans la même balance le monarque et le berger. . . ."
7. Ibid., I, 297. "Qu'est-ce qu'un roi? C'est un homme à qui le Ciel n'a pas donné une intelligence supérieure à celle d'un particulier et qui a des devoirs mille fois plus importants à remplir. . . ."
8. Ibid., I, 298. "Les institutions gothiques vont disparaître. Victor amènera par la main la vraie philosophie; il lui ordonnera de souffler sur les vieilles formules et l'ignorance, poursuivie, chassée, insultée dans toute l'Europe, ne se vantera plus que nous sommes ses derniers sujets."
9. Ibid., II, 46. "La vertu est une force constante, un état habituel de l'âme tout à fait indépendant des circonstances. . . ."
10. Ibid., II, 44. "Représentez-vous la naissance de la société; voyez ces hommes, las du pouvoir de tout faire, réunis en foule autour des autels sacrés

de la patrie qui vient de naître; tous abdiquent volontairement une partie de leur liberté; tous consentent à faire courber les volontés particulières sous le sceptre de la volonté générale: la hiérarchie sociale va se former. . . ."

11. Biographical data discussed in this section may be found in several sources. Among recent works the following are useful: Robert Triomphe, *Joseph de Maistre, Étude sur la vie et sur la doctrine d'un matérialiste mystique* (Geneva, 1968); Richard Allen Lebrun, *Throne and Altar, The Political and Religious Thought of Joseph de Maistre* (Ottawa, 1965).

12. Joseph de Maistre, *La Franc-Maçonnerie, Mémoire inédit au Duc de Brunswick* (1782), ed. Émile Dermenghem (Paris, 1925), p. 56. "Il y aurait des choses infinies à dire sur le caractère des vraies allégories, et sur l'excès de déraison où des écrivains d'ailleurs très estimables se sont vus entraînés par la fureur de chercher et d'expliquer des mystères."

13. Ibid., p. 58. ". . . une branche détachée et peut-être corrompue d'une tige ancienne respectable."

14. Ibid., p. 61. "Ne peut-on être utile et vertueux sans dévanciers? Nous sommes tous réunis au nom de la Religion et de l'humanité. Nous pouvons répondre de la droiture de nos intentions. Prenons hardiment l'édifice par les fondements et, au lieu de renouveler, créons."

15. Ibid., p. 107. "Comme, suivant la remarque de Pascal, les faux miracles prouvent les vrais, de même l'abus des explications allégoriques annonce que cette doctrine avait une racine réelle que nous avons perdue de vue."

Chapter Two

1. Unless otherwise mentioned the following edition will be referred to as *O. C.*: *Oeuvres complètes de Joseph de Maistre* (Lyon-Paris, 1884 - 1887), 14 Vols. "Nous sommes attachés au trône de l'Être suprême par une chaîne souple qui nous retient sans nous asservir" (I, 1).

2. Ibid., I, 3. "Mais dans les temps de révolutions, la chaîne qui lie l'homme se raccourcit brusquement . . . entraîné par une force inconnue, il se dépite contre elle, et au lieu de baiser la main qui le serre, il la méconnaît ou l'insulte."

3. Ibid., I, 7. "Au fond, c'était le *roi de la halle*. Par les crimes qu'il a faits . . . il a secondé le mouvement populaire. . . ."

4. Ibid., I, 18. "Le génie infernal de Robespierre pouvait seul opérer ce prodige. Le gouvernement révolutionnaire endurcissait l'âme des Français, en la trempant dans le sang."

5. Ibid., I, 19. "La magie noire qui opère dans ce moment, disparaîtrait comme un brouillard devant le soleil."

6. Ibid., I, 33. "Je ne pousserai pas plus loin cet épouvantable tableau; notre siècle et celui qui l'a précédé sont trop connus. Qu'on remonte jusqu'au berceau des nations; qu'on descende jusqu'à nos jours; qu'on examine les peuples dans toutes les positions possibles, depuis l'état de barbarie jusqu'à celui de la civilisation la plus raffinée on trouvera la guerre."

7. Ibid., I, 40. "Les spectateurs des grandes calamités humaines sont conduits surtout à ces tristes méditations. . . ."

8. Ibid., I, 55. "Il y a dans la révolution française un caractère satanique qui le distingue de tout ce qu'on a vu et peut-être de tout ce qu'on verra."

9. Ibid., I, 52. "Je vois l'ennemi du genre humain manège et convoquant tous les *mauvais esprits* dans ce nouveau *Pandaemonium*. . . ."

10. Ibid., I, 61. "Ou qu'il va se former une nouvelle religion ou que le Christianisme sera rajeuni de quelque manière extraordinaire. . . ."

11. Ibid., I, 111. "Mais que sommes-nous, faibles et aveugles humaines! et qu'est-ce que cette lumière tremblotante que nous appelons Raison?"

12. Ibid., I, 124 - 25. "Détrompez-vous une fois de ces doctrines désolantes, qui ont déshonoré notre siècle et perdu la France."

13. Ibid., I, 131. "Si l'on envisage la question sous un point de vue plus général, on trouvera que la monarchie est, sans contredit, le gouvernement qui donne le plus de distinction à un plus grand nombre de personnes."

14. Ibid., I, 145. "Le bonnet rouge, en touchant le front royal, a fait disparaître les traces de l'huile sainte; le charme est rompu. . . ."

15. Ibid., I, 155. "Le fanatisme de la liberté, échauffé par celui de la religion, y pénétra les âmes bien plus profondément qu'il ne l'a fait en France, où le culte de la liberté s'appuie sur le néant."

16. Ibid., I, 24. "En vérité, on serait tenté de croire que la révolution politique n'est qu'un objet secondaire du grand plan qui se déroule avant nous avec une majesté terrible."

17. Ibid., I, 28. "Le sang humain doit couler sans interruption sur le globe . . . la paix, pour chaque nation n'est qu'un répit."

18. Ibid., I, 39. "Il n'y a que violence dans l'univers; mais nous sommes gâtés par la philosophie moderne, qui a dit que *tout est bien*, tandis que le mal a tout souillé, et que, dans un sens très-vrai, tout est mal, puisque rien n'est à sa place."

19. Ibid., I, 61 - 62. "La génération présente est témoin de l'un des plus grands spectacles. . .le combat à outrance du Christianisme et du philosophisme. . . ."

20. Ibid., I, 65.

21. Ibid., I, 72. "Il y a entre la politique théorique et la législation constituante la même différence qui existe entre la poétique et la poésie. L'illustre Montesquieu est à Lycurgue, dans l'échelle générale des esprits, ce que Batteux est à Homère ou à Racine."

22. Ibid., I, 74.

23. Ibid., I, 118. "Non-seulement les peuples en masse n'entrent dans ces grands mouvements que comme le bois et les cordages employés par un machiniste; mais leurs chefs même ne sont tels que pour les yeux étrangers; dans le fait, ils sont dominés comme ils dominent le peuple. Ces hommes, qui, pris ensemble, semblent les tyrans de la multitude sont eux-mêmes tyrannisés par deux ou trois hommes, qui le sont par un seul. . . ."

24. Ibid., I, 2, 4. "Le *miracle* est un effet produit par une cause divine ou

sur-humaine . . . la révolution française, et tout ce qui se passe en Europe dans ce moment, est aussi merveilleux dans son genre que la fructification instantanée d'un arbre au mois de janvier. . . . Ce qui il y a de plus frappant dans la révolution française, c'est cette force entraînante qui courbe tous les obstacles. . . . La pureté des motifs a pu illustrer cet obstacle, mais c'est tout. . . ."

25. Ibid., I, 117. "Citoyens! voilà comment se font les contre-révolutions. Dieu . . . nous en avertit en ne confiant jamais à la multitude le choix de ses maîtres. Il ne l'emploie . . . que comme un instrument passif . . . le peuple romain se donna des maîtres en croyant combattre l'aristocratie à la suite de César. C'est l'image de toutes les insurrections populaires. . . ."

26. Ibid., I, 51. "Comment croire à la durée d'une liberté qui commence par la gangrène? . . ."

27. Ibid., I, 27. "L'horrible effusion du sang humain, occasionnée par cette grande commotion, est un moyen terrible. Cependant c'est un moyen autant qu'une punition, et il peut donner lieu à des réflexions intéressantes."

28. Ibid., I, 8. "Chaque nation, comme chaque individu, a reçu une mission qu'elle doit remplir. La France exerce sur l'Europe une véritable magistrature, qu'il serait inutile de contester. . . ."

29. Ibid., I, 10. "On nous cite l'Amérique; je ne connais rien de si impatientant que les louanges décernées à cet enfant au maillot; laissez-le grandir. . . . Non-seulement je ne crois point à la stabilité du gouvernement américain, mais les établissements particuliers de l'Amérique française ne m'inspirent aucune confidence. . . ."

30. See my *Lamartine* (New York, 1973).

31. *O. C.*, I, 56, 57. "En un mot, l'homme ne peut représenter le Créateur qu'en se mettant en rapport avec lui. Insensés que nous sommes, si nous voulons qu'un miroir réfléchisse l'image du soleil, le tournons-nous vers la terre? . . . Pour moi, je ne croirai jamais à la fécondité du néant."

32. Ibid., I, 191 - 92. "Pour exercer l'espèce de suprèmatie qui lui appartient, la France a reçu une langue dominatrice dont le caractère caché est encore un mystère, malgré tout ce qu'on a dit sur ce sujet."

33. Ibid., I, 192. "Les bons écrivains de cette nation expriment les choses mieux que ceux de toute nation, et font circuler leurs pensées dans toute l'Europe. . . ."

34. Ibid., I, 193. "Le trône de cette langue se trouvant placé entre le Nord et le Midi, elle se prête sans difficulté aux organes des autres peuples et devient pour eux un truchement universel et indispensable pour le commerce des pensées."

35. Ibid., I, 193. "C'est par l'ensemble qu'on frappe."

36. Ibid., I, 199. "Les arts, qui sont l'expression du génie des peuples, peignaient la corruption générale."

37. Ibid., I, 235. "Une des grandes erreurs du siècle qui les professa toutes, fut de croire qu'une constitution publique pouvait être écrite et créée *a priori*, tandis que la raison et l'expérience se réunissent pour établir qu'une

constitution est une oeuvre divine, et que ce qu'il y a précisément de plus fondamental et de plus essentiellement constitutionnel dans les lois d'une nation ne saurait être écrit."

38. Ibid., I, 236 - 37.

39. Ibid., I, 241. "La véritable *constitution anglaise* est cet esprit public admirable, unique, infaillible, au-dessus de tout éloge. . . . On ne conçoit pas comment un homme sensé peut rêver la possibilité d'une pareille chimère."

40. Ibid., I, 231. "L'homme ne peut faire de souverain. Tout au plus, il peut servir d'instrument pour déposséder un souverain et livrer ses États à un autre souverain déjà prince. . . ."

41. Ibid., I, 243, 247 - 48. "Le dix-huitième siècle, qui ne s'est douté de rien, n'a douté de rien." "La plus grande folie, peut-être, du siècle des folies, fut de croire que des lois fondamentales pouvaient être écrites *a priori*. . . ."

42. Ibid., I, 243. "Or, je le dis sans le moindre esprit de contention, et sans prétendre choquer personne, ils montrent en cela autant de philosophie et de véritable savoir que s'ils cherchaient dans un enfant au maillot les véritables dimensions de l'homme. . . ."

43. Ibid., I, 285. "Plus elle sera pénétrée par le principe divin, plus elle sera durable."

44. Ibid., I, 286. "Hélas! il n'a fini que dans nos almanachs."

45. Ibid., I, 304. "Il a combattu le matérialisme dans l'article LEUCIPPE de son dictionnaire. . . ."

46. Ibid., I, 311. "Le peuple est souverain, dit-on; et de qui?—De lui-même apparemment. . . ."

47. Ibid., I, 315. "C'est une manie étrange de l'homme de se créer des difficultés pour avoir le plaisir de les résoudre. . . ."

48. Ibid., I, 318. "Ce mot, dans son acception la plus étendue, ne signifie réellement que l'ensemble de toutes des lois, de toutes les forces, et de tous les ressorts *qui constituent* l'univers. . . ."

49. Ibid., I, 321. "L'art est la nature de l'homme. . . ."

50. Ibid., I, 327. "Les autres mécontents du royaume, quoiqu'en beaucoup plus grand nombre, n'ont pu opérer rien de pareil parce que ces mécontents ne sont que des *hommes,* au lieu que la Vendée est une *nation.* . . ."

51. Ibid., I, 341. "Tout est bon dans ses ouvrages, excepté ses systèmes."

52. Ibid., I, 441. "C'est au milieu des forêts et des glâces du Nord que nos gouvernements ont pris naissance. C'est là qu'est né le caractère européen. . . ."

53. Ibid., I, 410. "Une goutte de cet océan incommensurable d'existence semble se détacher et tomber sur l'homme qui parle et agit au nom de la divinité. . . ."

Chapter Three

1. Unpublished letter quoted in Triomphe, *Joseph de Maistre*, p. 333.

"Je me croirais même en état de faire comprendre à une société d'athées qu'ils ont sur ce point le même intérêt que nous. . . ."

2. *O. C.*, II, xii. "Les mots de souveraineté et d'infaillibilité sont deux synonymes naturels. . . ."

3. Ibid., II, xvii, xix, xx. "Notre ordre s'est rendue, pendant le dernier siècle, éminemment coupable envers la Religion. . . . l'Église recommence . . . il pourra nous étonner par sa science. . . . Nous touchons à la plus grande des époques religieuses. . . ."

4. Ibid., II, 2. "Nous demandons seulement qu'elle jouisse du droit commun à toutes les souverainetés possibles qui toutes agissent nécessairement comme infaillibles. . . ."

5. Ibid., II, 29. "Si l'on ôte de ce morceau l'insulte et le ton de scurrilité . . . il reste quelque chose de vrai; plus le monde sera éclairé, et moins on pensera à un concile général. . . ."

6. Ibid., II, 132. "La correspondance mystérieuse entre les langues et les signes de l'écriture est telle, que si une langue balbutie, l'écriture balbutiera de même; que si la langue est vague, embarrassée et d'une syntaxe difficile, l'écriture manquera de même, et proportionnellement d'élégance et de clarté."

7. Ibid., II, 83. "Quelles toiles d'araignées; quelles subtilités indignes de Bossuet! . . ."

8. Ibid., II, 162. "Qu'on jette les yeux sur une mappe-monde, qu'on trace la ligne où *cette langue universelle* se tut; là sont les bornes de la civilisation et de la fraternité européennes . . . les Français . . . oublièrent presque entièrement cette langue; ils se sont oubliés eux-mêmes jusqu'à la faire disparaître de leur monnaie. . . ."

9. Ibid., II, 305. "Quant aux guerres justes, saintes même et nécessaires, telles que les croisades, si les Papes les ont provoquées et soutenues de tout leur pouvoir, ils ont bien fait, et nous leur en devons d'immortelles d'actions de grâces. . . ."

10. Ibid., II, 172. "Un certain esprit soldatesque, qui est la gangrène de la liberté, menace assez visiblement la constitution anglaise; je passe volontiers sous silence d'autres symptômes. . . ."

11. Ibid., II, 173. "Le protestantisme, au contraire, partant de la souveraineté du peuple, dogme qu'il a transporté de la religion dans la politique, ne voit, dans le système de la non-résistance, que le dernier avilissement de l'homme. . . ."

12. Ibid., II, 338 - 39. "Aristote est même allé . . . jusqu'à dire *qu'il y avait des hommes qui naissaient esclaves.* . . . Celui qui a suffisamment étudié cette triste nature, sait que l'homme en général, s'il s'est réduit à lui-même, *est trop méchant pour être libre.*"

13. Ibid., II, 345. "La femme est plus que l'homme redevable au Christianisme. C'est de lui qu'elle tient toute sa dignité. La femme chrétienne est vraiment un être *surnaturel*, puisqu'elle est soulevée, maintenue par lui jusqu'à un état qui ne lui est pas *naturel*. Mais par quels services immenses elle paye cette espèce d'ennoblissement!

14. Ibid., II, 425. "Un beau phénomène est celui de la. Russie. Placée entre l'Europe et l'Asie elle tient de l'une et de l'autre. L'élément asiatique qu'elle possède et qui saute aux yeux, ne doit point l'humilier. On pourrait y voir plutôt un titre de supériorité. . . ."

15. Ibid., III, 27. "Quelques sectaires mélancoliques, aigris par les poursuites de l'autorité, imaginèrent de s'enfermer dans une solitude pour y bouder et y travailler à l'aise. . . . L'orgueil, le ressentiment, la rancune religieuse, toutes les passions aigres et haineuses se déchaînent à la fois. L'esprit de parti concentré se transforme en rage incurable. . . ."

16. Ibid., III, 60 - 61.

17. Ibid., III, 80.

18. Ibid., III, 29. "Le reste ne vaut pas l'honneur d'être nommé. . . ."

19. Ibid., III, 21. "La plume élégante de Mme. de Sévigné confirme parfaitement . . . en croyant faire un panégyrique, l'atrocité des dogmes jansénistes, l'hypocrisie de la secte et la subtilité de ses manoeuvres. Cette secte . . . est encore la plus vile à cause du caractère de fausseté qui la distingue. . . ."

20. Ibid., III, 33. "Port-Royal s'empara du temps et des facultés d'un assez grand nombre d'écrivains qui pouvaient se rendre utiles . . . divisa l'Église . . . aigrit les esprits et les accoutuma à la résistance; il fomenta le soupçon et l'antipathie. . . ."

21. Ibid., III, 37. "Non seulement les talents furent médiocres à *Port-Royal*, mais le cercle de ces talents fut extrêmement restreint, non seulement dans les sciences proprement dites, mais encore dans ce genre de connaissances qui se rapportaient le plus particulièrement à leur état. . . ."

22. Ibid., III, 40. "Mais rien n'augmenta la puissance de Port-Royal sur l'opinion public, comme l'usage exclusif qu'ils firent de la langue française dans tous leurs écrits. Ils savaient le grec sans doute, ils savaient le latin, mais sans être ni hellénistes, ni latinistes, ce qui est bien différent . . . ils n'ont pas même su faire l'épitaphe de Pascal en bon latin. . . ."

23. Ibid., III, 47. "La Harpe m'étonne fort lorsque, dans je ne sais quel endroit de son Lycée, il décide *que les solitaires de Port-Royal furent très-superieurs aux Jésuites dans la composition des livres élémentaires.* Je n'examine pas si les Jésuites furent créés pour composer des grammaires . . . mais quand cette petite supériorité vaudrait la peine d'être disputée. . . ."

24. Ibid., III, 53. "Pascal passa quatre ou cinq ans de sa vie dans les murs de Port-Royal, dont il devint la gloire sans lui devoir rien; mais quoique je ne veuille nullement déroger à son mérite réel qui est très-grand, il faut avouer aussi qu'il a été trop loué. . . ."

25. Ibid., III, 154 - 55. " . . . Bousset entra dans l'assemblée comme modérateur. . . . Il ne voulait point qu'on y traitât de l'autorité du Pape; cette épouvantable imprudence devait choquer à l'excès un homme dont la qualité la plus saillante était la crainte de se compromettre avec aucune autorité. . . ."

26. Ibid., III, 318 - 19. "Une jeune fille, innocente, brulée dans une grande capitale de l'Europe, sans autre crime que de croire à sa religion

serait un forfait national si horrible, qu'il suffirait pour flétrir un people et peut-être un siècle entier. . . ."

Chapter Four

1. Triomphe, *Joseph de Maistre*, pp. 577 - 85.

2. Ibid., IV, 73. "Ne confondons pas les termes: ceux de *conversation,* de *dialogue* et *d'entretien* ne sont pas synonymes. La *conversation* divague de sa nature. . . . Mais l'entretien est beaucoup plus sage . . . l'entretien est subordonné aux règles de l'art dramatique qui n'admettent point un quatrième interlocuteur. . . . Quant au *dialogue,* ce mot ne représente qu'une fiction; car il suppose une conversation qui n'a jamais existé. . . ."

3. Ibid., IV, 3. "Son disque environné de vapeurs rougeâtres roule comme un char enflammé sur les sombres forêts qui couronnent l'horizon, et ses rayons réfléchis par le vitrage des palais, donnent au spectateur l'idée d'un vaste incendie. . . ."

4. Ibid., V, 6 - 7. "Le militaire et le bourreau occupent en effet les deux extrémités de l'échelle sociale. . . . Il n'y a rien de si noble que le premier, rien de si abject que le second. . . ."

5. Ibid., IV, 33 - 34. "Ôtez du monde cet agent incompréhensible; dans l'instant même l'ordre fait place au chaos. . . . Il y a donc dans le cercle temporel une loi divine et visible pour la punition du crime, et cette loi. . . . est exécutée invariablement depuis l'origine des choses. . . ."

6. Ibid., V, 283 - 360. See *Éclaricissement sur les sacrifices.*

7. Ibid., IV, 25. "*Le mal physique n'a pu entrer dans l'univers que par la faute des créatures libres; il ne peut y être que comme remède ou expiation, et par conséquent il ne peut avoir Dieu pour auteur direct. . . .*"

8. Ibid., IV, 282. "La philosophie du dernier siècle . . . n'a rien oublié pour nous détourner de la prière par la considération *des lois éternelles et immuables. . . .*"

9. Ibid., V, 56. "La lumière intimide le vice; la nuit lui rend toutes ses forces, c'est la vertu qui a peur. . . ."

10. Ibid., V, 57. "C'est l'époque des profondes méditations et des sublimes ravissements; pour mettre à profits ces élans divins . . . le Christianisme s'est emparé à son tour de la nuit, et l'a consacrée à de saintes cérémonies qu'il anime par une musique austère et de puissants cantiques. . . ."

11. Ibid., IV, 109. "Il n'en est pas, je crois, de plus avillissant, de plus funeste pour l'esprit humain. Par lui la raison a perdu ses ailes, et se traîne comme un reptile fangeux; par lui fut tarie la source divine de la poésie et de l'éloquence. . . ."

12. Ibid., IV, 319. "Quelle odeur de magasin! . . ."

13. Ibid., IV, 87. "Nulle langue n'a pu être inventée, ni par un homme qui n'aurait pu se faire obéir, ni par plusieurs qui n'auraient pu s'entendre. . . . *Il s'est élancé avant tous les temps du sein de son principe; il est aussi ancien que l'éternité . . . Qui pourra raconter son origine? . . .*"

14. Ibid., IV, 46. "Les sages de l'antiquité, quoique privés des lumières que nous possédons, étaient cependant plus près de l'origine des choses, et quelques restes des traditions primitives étaient descendus jusqu'à eux. . . ."
15. Ibid., IV, 56.
16. Ibid., IV, 14. "C'est une de mes idées favorites que l'homme droit est assez communément averti; par un sentiment intérieur, de la fausseté ou de la vérité de certaines propositions avant tout examen, souvent même sans avoir fait les études nécessaires pour être en état de les examiner. . . ."
17. Ibid., IV, 56.
18. Ibid., V, 118. "Souvent aussi j'y place ces pénsées du moment; ces *illuminations soudaines* qui s'éteignent sans fruit si l'éclair n'est pas fixé par l'écriture. . . . Chaque passage réveille dans moi une foule d'idées intéressantes et de souvenirs mélancoliques. . . ."
19. Ibid., IV, 379. "Young, Richardson, etc., n'ont été connus et goûtés en Europe que par les traductions et les recommandations françaises."
20. Ibid., IV, 97. "Il sait *répandre* la voix divine autour de l'oreille humaine, comme une atmosphère sonore qui résonne encore après que le Dieu a cessé de parler."
21. Ibid., V, 45. "S'il descend aux phénomènes particuliers, quelle abondance d'images! quelle richesse d'expressions! Voyez avec quelle vigueur et quelle grâce il exprime les *noces* de la terre et de l'élément humide. . . ."
22. Ibid., V, 92. "L'inépuisable imagination de Roland a pu couvrir sa fameuse galerie d'assemblages fantastiques; mais chaque pièce existe dans la nature. . . ."
23. Ibid., IV, 211, 314, 213, 282. "La prière est la respiration de l'âme." "Toute prière légitime . . . comme une rosée bienfaisante qui nous prépare pour une autre patrie. . . ." "L'homme, malgré sa dégradation porte toujours des marques évidentes de son origine divine. . . ." "La prière est la dynamique confiée à l'homme. . . ."
24. Ibid., V, 190. "*Que le chimiste imprudent court risque d'adorer son ouvrage.*"
25. Ibid., V, 195 - 96. "La superstition n'est donc ni l'erreur ni le fanatisme. . . . Ce sera donc quelque chose qui est *par delà* la croyance légitime. . . . En vérité, il n'y a pas de quoi crier *haro*. . . . En amour, en amitié, en fidélité . . . la supersition est aimable, précieuse même et souvent nécessaire; pourquoi n'en serait-il de même de la piété? . . ."
26. Ibid., IV, 254, 200. "L'ordre temporel est . . . l'image d'un ordre supérieur. . . ."
27. Ibid., V, 118. "Chaque passage réveille dans moi une foule d'idées intéressantes et de souvenirs mélancoliques mille fois plus doux que tout ce qu'on est convenu d'appeler *plaisirs*. . . ."
28. Ibid., V, 234. "Le prophète jouissant du privilège de sortir du temps, ses idées n'étant plus distribuées dans la durée. . . ."
29. Ibid., V, 235. "L'esprit prophétique est naturel à l'homme, et ne cessera de s'agiter dans le monde. L'homme, en essayant, à toutes les époques et dans tous les lieux, de pénétrer dans l'avenir, déclare qu'il n'est pas

fait pour le temps; car le temps est quelque chose de forcé et ne demande qu'à finir. De là vient que dans nos songes, jamais nous n'avons l'idée du temps, et que l'état du sommeil fut toujours jugé favorable aux communications divines. . . ."

30. Ibid., V, 237 - 38. "Celui-là sera fameux, et mettra fin au XVIIIe siècle qui dure toujours; car les siècles intellectuels ne se réglent pas sur le calendrier comme les *siècles* proprement dits. Alors des opinions, qui nous paraissent aujourd'hui bizarres ou insensées, seront des axiomes dont il ne sera pas permis de douter; et l'on parlera de notre *stupidité* actuelle, comme nous parlons de la superstition du moyen âge. . . ."

31. Ibid., V, 242. "Et ne dites point que tout est dit, que tout est révélé, et qu'il ne nous est permis d'attendre rien de nouveau . . . du côté des connaissances divines, il nous manque beaucoup, et quant aux manifestations futures, j'ai, comme vous voyez, mille raisons pous m'y attendre. . . ."

32. Dermenghem, *Joseph de Maistre, mystique*, pp. 44 - 45.

33. Louis-Claude de Saint-Martin, *L'Homme de désir* (Lyon, 1790), p. 28. "Oh! combien la realité du monde futur sera belle à nos yeux, puisque l'illusion de ce monde actuel . . . est si imposante et si magnifique!"

34. Ibid., pp. 14, 164. Quand ton coeur est plein de Dieu, emploie la prière verbale. . . . Quand ton coeur sera sec et vide, emploie la prière muette et concentrée. . . . Elle est une seule ressource . . . dans cette région ténébreuse et sur ce misérable théâtre d'expiation."

35. Ibid., p. 28. "L'homme régénéré y promène ses regards sans interruption sur les êtres vivants et purs, dont l'aspect le sanctifie."

36. Ibid., p. 2. "Des preuves irrésistibles sur les vérités premières n'ont-elles pas déjà été manifestées aux nations?"

37. Ibid., p. 44. "Ils ne connaissent pas même encore l'origine de leurs droits publiques et terrestres; cependant ils ne s'empressent pas moins de se préscrire des lois qu'ils croient justes, dès que leurs voix sont comptées."

38. Ibid., p. 128. "Réfléchis à ces témoins irrésistibles, et nie si tu peux, un crime originel."

39. Ibid., p. 151. "Le criminel qui n'a rien fait aux bourreaux, pourrait leur dire que c'est avec injustice qu'ils le tourmentent, puisqu'il ne leur a rien fait; mais il sent que c'est avec justice qu'il est dévoué au supplice et à la mort."

40. Ibid., p. 206. "Est-ce que nous devions avoir des souffrances d'expiation? Ne ne devions avoir que des souffrances de sacrifices; parce que la charité seule devait animer tous les êtres, et qu'ils ne devaient avoir d'autre emploi que de travailler au rétablissement de l'alliance."

41. Ibid., pp. 13, 141, 275. "La parole avait été nécessaire à l'institution de la parole. . . . L'homme l'avait recue, cette parole, il avait été choisi pour être le chantre de Dieu et pour en célébrer toutes les merveilles. . . . Serait-il donc vrai que c'est en écrivant que l'on a perdu les langues?"

42. See my *Lamartine* (New York, 1973).

43. *L'Homme de désir*, p. 377. "Mais la poésie épique ne peut se passer

de la poésie prophétique, la seule vraiment puissante et capable de suffire à tous les bésoins légitimes de notre esprit. . . ."

44. *Ibid.,* p. 373. "Homme de désir, vas-y seul comme le grand prêtre. . . ."

45. See footnote eleven.

Chapter Five

1. *O. C.,* V, 302. "Toujours la victime était brûlée en tout ou en partie, pour attester que la peine naturelle du crime est le feu, et que la *chair sub-stituée* était brulée à la place de la *chair coupable.*"

2. *Ibid.,* V, 284. "La musique, la poésie, la danse, en un mot tous les arts agréables, étaient appelés aux cérémonies du culte. . . ."

3. *Ibid.,* V, 293 - 94. "Milton a mis de beaux vers dans la bouche de Satan, qui rugit de son épouvantable dégradation. . . ."

4. *Ibid.,* VI, 4. "Rarement il résiste à l'envie d'être poéte."

5. *Ibid.,* VI, 43. "Son style est, pour ainsi dire, matériel; il ne s'exerce que sur les formes, sur les masses, sur les mouvements. Sa pensée semble . . . *se corporiser et s'incorporer* avec les objets qui l'occupaient uniquement. . . . Il n'y a pas dans toutes ses oeuvres une ligne, un mot qui s'adresse à l'esprit; celui de *nature* ou d'*essence,* par exemple, le choque; il aime mieux dire *forme* parce qu'il la voit. . . ."

6. *Ibid.,* VI, 84. "Le charlatan est pris en flagrant délit; *il change les termes.* . . . Il voulait nous enseigner à chercher l'essence, et il nous parle de *qualités.* C'est abuser du langage pour se tromper et pour tromper. . . . Que signifie ce galimatias? . . ."

7. *Ibid.,* VI, 277. "Chaque ligne de Bacon conduit au matérialisme; mais nulle part il ne s'est montré plus habile sophiste, hypocrite plus raffiné . . . que dans ce qu'il a écrit sur l'âme."

8. *Ibid.,* VI, 293. "Ainsi l'homme est *lumière et fontaine,* feu follet et torrent. . . . La lumière est moins brillante, une fontaine est moins claire, un feu follet est moins subtil, un torrent moins entraînant que cette tirade élo-quente."

9. *Ibid.,* VI, 456 - 57. "Il est encore très important de remarquer qu'indépendamment de la supériorité du dix-septième siècle dans les ouvrages philosophiques proprement dits, sa littérature entière . . . respire je ne sais quelle philosophie sage . . . qui, s'adressant constamment au bon sens universel ne surprend, ne choque, et ne trouble personne. Ce tact exquis, cette mesure parfaite fut nommée timidité par le siècle suivant, qui n'estima que la contradiction, l'audace et l'exagération."

10. *Ibid.,* VII, 147. "Oh! saintes et divines lois, émanations célestes! honneur de la nature humaine! C'est par vous, seulement, que les Souverains se rapprochent de leur modèle. Lorsqu'on se recueille un instant, et qu'on réfléchit sur les merveilles de l'organisation politique, on croit entendre la voix de la Divinité même. . . ."

11. Ibid., VII, 248. "Oh ma patrie! ô peuple infortuné! Comment pourras-tu pleurer assez le voisinage funeste qui a versé sur toi un déluge de maux! Heureux mille fois le Lapon au milieu de ses glâces éternelles! heureux l'Arabe bédouin sur sa terre échorchée par un soleil brûlant! . . ."

12. Ibid., VII, 291. "Rousseau, raisonnant sur ce point, a pensé . . . que pour détruire des duels, il faudrait les permettre. . . . Louis XIV . . . avait imaginé . . . sa classification des impertinences . . . pour l'épithète de *faquin*, tant d'années en prison . . . pour celle de *poltron*, tant, etc. . . ."

13. Ibid., VII, 291. "Je voudrais fondre les deux projets, pour en former une troisième . . . le *nec plus ultra* de la législation."

14. Ibid., VII, 297. "Accoutumés de bonne heure à ne rien refuser à une femme, à ne la contrarier sur rien et à lui passer tout, il n'y a pas de raison d'agir autrement parce qu'elle est reine."

15. Ibid., VII, 298. "Certes, c'est un spectacle bien honorable pour les femmes, de voir tous les projets de Pierre le Grand, couvés par des jupons, éclore majestueusement aux yeux de l'Europe étonnée. . . ."

16. Ibid., VII, 300. "Ce qu'on appelle le *caractère* d'un homme n'est qu'un assemblage de *tics*, et le *tic* n'est qu'un fils de l'habitude. . . ."

17. Ibid., VII, 339. "Ce théorème de *trigonométrie* ne choque point les esprits les plus justes de l'Europe."

18. Ibid., VII, 340. "Les autres poètes ont peint une nature idéale, Shakespeare seul a peint une nature vraie, une nature générale, en un mot, une nature *naturelle*."

19. Ibid., VII, 347. "Il est clair que toutes les questions de goût doivent se décider . . . à la pluralité. . . ."

20. Ibid., VII, 474. "Non-seulement la Révolution a porté un coup sensible aux arts en détruisant ou exilant un nombre infini de chefs d'oeuvre dans tous les genres; elle leur a fait encore une plaie bien plus profonde par l'espèce d'homme qu'elle a porté au pouvoir et à l'influence. . . ."

21. Ibid., VII, 510. "Rousseau s'empara de ce sujet fait exprès pour lui. Tout ce qui était obscur, tout ce qui ne présentait aucun sens déterminé, tout ce qui prêtait aux divagations et aux équivoques était particulièrement de son domaine."

22. Ibid., VIII, 23. "L'éditeur possède un talent merveilleux pour réunir constamment un barbarisme à une pensée fausse. . . ." "M. Grouvelle est le premier homme sans goût et sans talent, le premier écrivain détestable que nous ayons vu se passionner pour ces lettres. . . ."

23. Ibid., VIII, 31. "On dirait qu'il a toujours à côté de lui un méchant lutin qui lui souffle les expressions les plus baroques. . . ."

24. Ibid., VIII, 359. "Tout ce qui a été dit est fondé sur l'expérience, sur la connaissance intime des hommes, du siècle, des circonstances, et de la Russie en particulier. Chaque assertion est appuyée sur des témoignages incontestables, tous arrachés aux accusés *par la torture de la vérité*. . . ."

25. Ibid., VIII, 487. "La Révolution française ne fut qu'une suite directe, une conclusion visible et inévitable des principes posés dans le seizième et

dans le dix-huitième siècle; et maintenant l'état de l'Europe est tel, qu'il laisse craindre encore les plus violentes convulsions."

Chapter Six

1. *O. C.*, IX, 1. To M.——, February 20, 1786: "J'ai trouvé sa réputation prodigieusement exagérée, comme tout ce que vient de France."

2. Ibid., IX, 2 - 3. To M.——, February 20, 1786: "Les poètes durs sont précisément ceux qu'elle rend le mieux. Elle ne sait pas déclamer Racine, elle rend mieux Voltaire, parce qu'il est plus sentencieux et moins naturel. Elle ne nous a rien donné de Corneille, ni de Crébillon, parce qu'apparemment ces petits écrivains ne sont pas dignes de son talent. . . . Malgré tous ces défauts, votre belle soeur peut passer pour une grande actrice, pourvu qu'elle ne sorte pas de son genre. Elle exprime fort bien la fureur, la jalousie, le désespoir, en un mot tous les sentiments fougueux et déchirants; il faudrait seulement l'avertir de ne pas s'emporter, car alors elle hurle et fatigue l'oreille. . . . Le cri qu'elle fit lorsqu'elle reconnut Raoul . . . était celui de la nature, et il résonne encore dans mon oreille; enfin elle me donna une idée de la perfection. . . . Conclusion: son talent est grand, mais mêlé de grands défauts. . . ."

3. Ibid., IX, 9. To Mlle Thérèse de Maistre, July 12, 1790: "Je m'engage à soutenir son orthodoxie sur tous les chefs, même sur celui de l'assemblée nationale, qu'il condamne clairement."

4. Ibid., IX, 29. To M. le Comte Henri Costa de Beauregard, April 27, 1792: "Quel siècle, grand Dieu, ou pour mieux dire, quelle nation! Comparez la conduite des Anglais à l'égard du malheureux Charles Ier: vous verrez que les Français sont inférieurs à leurs rivaux par les crimes, autant que par les grandes actions, et que la première nation est à la deuxième . . . ce que l'hyène est au lion."

5. Ibid., IX, 84. To M. le Baron Vignet des Étoles, December 23, 1794: "Ma correspondance devient, elle seule, un ouvrage immense. . . ."

6. Ibid., IX, 104. To M. le Comte Napione Coconato, January 20, 1802: "Je n'accepte point le compliment que vous me faites sur ma philosophie. Ce que nous appelons de ce beau nom n'est le plus souvent qu'un simple tempérament. Dans moi, ce ne peut être qu'un peu de ce génie Gallican qui déconcerte parfois le malheur, en lui riant au nez. . . ."

7. Ibid., IX, 189. To M. le Chevalier de Rossi, Saint-Petersburg, July 1804: "Les Bourbons français ne sont certainement inférieurs à aucune race régnante; ils ont beaucoup d'esprit et de bonté . . . nullement capables de la rétablir. . . ."

8. Ibid. IX, 193. To M. le Chevalier de Rossi, Saint-Petersburg, July 1804: "Je me crois donc bien fondé à croire que la commission de Bonaparte est de rétablir la monarchie, et d'ouvrir tous les yeux, en irritant également les royalistes et les Jacobins; après quoi il disparaîtra. . . ."

9. Ibid., IX, 201 - 2. To Mlle. Adèle de Maistre, Saint-Petersburg, April 12, 1804: "Je loue beaucoup ton goût pour le Tasse. . . ."

10. Ibid., IX, 305. To Mlle. Adèle de Maistre, Saint-Petersburg, 1804; "Qu'il se les mette dans la tête, surtout l'inimitable Racine; n'importe qu'il ne le comprenne pas encore. . . ."

11. Ibid, IX, 302. To Mlle. Adèle de Maistre, Saint-Petersburg, December 26, 1804: "Crois-tu que ce grand comique, ce juge infallible de ridicules, eût traité ce sujet, s'il n'avait pas reconnu que le titre de femme savante est en effet un ridicule? Le plus grand défaut pour une femme, *c'est d'être homme.* Pour écarter jusqua'à l'idée de cette prétention défavorable, il faut absolument obéir à Salomon, à Fénelon, et à Molière; ce trio est infaillible. . . ."

12. Ibid., IX, 443 - 44. To Mme la Marquise de Priero, August 1805: "C'est donc vous . . . qui avez promené *la Science en jupon!* Je vous en félicite, et je suis charmé que vous ayez pu, comme moi, examiner de près cette femme célèbre, ou fameuse, qui aurait pu être adorable, et qui a voulu n'être qu'extraordinaire. Il ne faut pas disputer des gouts, mais suivant le mien, elle s'est bien trompée. . . . Elle dit fort bien ce qu'elle veut dire. Je ne connais pas de tête aussi complètement pervertie; c'est l'opération infaillible de la philosophie moderne sur toute femme quelconque, mais le coeur n'est pas mauvais du tout. A cet égard, on lui a fait tort. Quant à l'esprit, elle en a prodigieusement, surtout . . . lorsqu'elle ne cherche pas à en avoir. N'ayant étudié ensemble ni en théologie ni en politique, nous avons donné en Suisse des scènes à mourir de rire, cependant sans nous brouiller jamais. . . ."

13. Ibid., IX, 265. To M. le Comte d'Avaray, Saint-Petersburg, 1804: "Je vous avoue qu'il s'élève dans mon coeur certains mouvements qui me font balancer, malgré la détermination absolue de la raison. Je me dis comme Montaigne! Que sais-je? Il arrive des événements si extraordinaries! . . ."

14. Ibid., IX. To M. le Chevalier de Rossi, Saint-Petersburg, May 29, 1805: "Ils sont lâches sans obéissance, et rebelles sans courage. Ils ont des études sans science, une jurisprudence sans justice, et un culte sans religion. . . . Le Sarde est plus sauvage que le sauvage, car le sauvage ne connaît pas la lumière, et le Sarde la hait. . . ."

15. Ibid., X, 5. *Mémoire.* Saint-Petersburg, December 21, 1805: "Les haines nationales ne produisent que du mal."

16. Ibid., X, 105, 107. To M. le Chevalier de Rossi, April 14, 1806: "Tout homme qui ne met pas sa mort au rang des événements possibles à chaque instant, n'a pas fait de grands progrès dans la philosophie. . . . " "Cette philosophie qui dépend malheureusement bien plus du tempérament que de la raison."

17. Ibid., X, 171. To M. le Baron de Pauliani, Saint-Petersburg, July 28, 1806: "L'homme n'a que les rêves; il n'est lui-même qu'un rêve. . . ."

18. Ibid., X, 213. To Mlle Adèle de Maistre, October 8, 1806: "Ma vie s'ecoule tristement. Je regarde les minutes qui tombent l'une après l'autre dans l'eternité; je les compte, je les assemble, j'en fais des heures et des jours, sans éprouver jamais qu'amertume. Á mon âge toutes les illusions sont finies; il ne reste que la famille, et c'est ce qui me manque. . . ."

19. Ibid., X, 261. To Mme la Comtesse de la Chavanne, Saint-Petersburg, November 10, 1806: "Les autres coeurs me sont étrangers. . . ."

20. Ibid., X, 295 - 96. To Mlle Adèle de Maistre, Saint-Petersburg, January 7, 1807: "Aucun juge sage et instruit ne pardonnera à Alfieri d'avoir falsifié l'histoire pour satisfaire l'extravagance et les préjugés stupides du dix-huitième siècle."

21. Ibid., X, 112. To Monseigneur de la Fare, Saint-Petersburg, May 13, 1806: "Il y a longtemps . . . que je roule dans ma tête certains dialogues sur la Providence, où je ferais voir assez clairement, je pense, que toutes ces plaintes tant rebattues de l'impunité du crime ne sont que des ignorances et des sophismes. . . ."

22. Ibid., 150 - 51. To M. le Chevalier de Rossi, July 5, 1806: "Or je vous demande si parmi cette foule de capitaines et de politiques qui s'évertuent de notre côté, il en est qu'on puisse mettre en équilibre avec Bonaparte et sa bande. . . . Ce qui se prépare maintenant dans le monde est un des plus merveilleux spectacles que la Providence ait jamais donnés aux hommes, mais le développement de ce plan est le sujet d'un livre, non d'une lettre. . . ."

23. Ibid., X, 440. To M. le Comte d'Avaray, Saint-Petersburg, July, 12, 1807: "Il n'y a plus de poésie dans le monde. . . . Il n'y a plus de religion ni d'amour; mais si jamais elle renaît, la Révolution française formera le plus noble sujet d'un poème épique. Les longues erreurs de votre Maître formeront un riche épisode de ce poème."

24. Ibid., XI, 3. To M. le Chevalier de Rossi, Saint-Petersburg, January 4, 1808: "La médiocrité des personnes par qui de si grandes choses s'exécutent. . . ."

25. Ibid., XI, 100. To M. le Chevalier de Rossi, Saint-Petersburg, May, 1808: "Si je pouvais aborder Napoléon, j'aurais des moyens d'adoucir le lion. . . ."

26. Ibid., XI, 109. To M. le Chevalier de Rossi, Saint-Petersburg, May, 1808: "Peut-être n'étais-je bon que pour la vie patriarcale. . . . La Révolution en a ordonné autrement. . . ."

27. Ibid., XI, 170. To M. le Chevalier de Rossi, Saint-Petersburg, November 10, 1808: "L'Empereur *me passa à peu près sous silence.* . . . en présence des *maîtres* il n'ose pas être poli. . . ."

28. Ibid., XI, 263 - 65. To Mlle. Adèle de Maistre, Saint-Petersburg, July 11, 1809: "Voilà pourquoi Voltaire n'a jamais pu faire une comédie; il fait rire les lèvres, mais le rire du coeur, celui qu'on appelle le bon rire, ne peut être éprouvé ni excité que par les bonnes gens. . . ."

29. Ibid., XI, 142. To Mlle. Constance de Maistre, Saint-Petersburg, October 24, 1808: "Il est assez plaisant que ceux qui ne les savent pas veuillent absolument prouver le vice des méthodes employées par nous qui les savons. . . ."

30. Ibid., XI, 148. To Mlle. Constance de Maistre, Saint-Petersburg, 1808: "Le mérite de la femme est de régler sa maison, de rendre son mari heureux, de le consoler, de l'encourager, et d'élever ses enfants, c'est-à-dire *de faire des hommes.* . . ."

31. Ibid., XI, 421 - 22. To Mlle. Adèle de Maistre, Saint-Petersburg,

March 13, 1810: "J'imagine que tu ne veux pas parler des triumvirs du grand siècle: Lebrun, Lesueur, le Poussin. Ces trois-là en valent bien d'autres. Le troisième surtout (à la vérité tout à fait *italianisé*) est mon héroes; il n'y a pas de peinture que je comprenne mieux. Quant aux artistes modernes français, je te les livre. . . ."

32. Ibid., XI, 520. To M. le Chevalier de Rossi, Saint Petersburg, December 7, 1810: "Leur civilisation au lieu de s'opérer graduellement comme la nôtre, s'est opérée brusquement. . . . les circonstances ont mis le Russe en contact avec une nation qui était à la fois l'orne le plus actif et la plus déplorable victime de cette corruption. . . ."

33. Ibid., XII, 201. To M. le Comte de Front, Saint-Petersburg, September 2, 1812: "Kutusoff est un homme de soixante-dix ans au moins, gros et pesant, plein d'esprit d'ailleurs, et fin à l'excès . . . il est défiguré par une blessure épouvantable; une balle lui perça la tête jadis obliquement et sortit par la cavité de l'oeil. Le globe est déplacé et l'autre oeil même a beaucoup souffert. . . ."

34. Ibid., XII, 206 - 7. To M. le Comte de Front, Saint-Petersburg, September 2, 1812: "Napoléon perd évidemment la tête en s'avançant ainsi qu'il le fait; il ne peut plus être sauvé, ce me semble, que par son étoile, mais, quand on se fie aux étoiles, à la fin on est dupe. . . . Tout en faisant sonner la trompette dans toute l'Europe, il est sûrement fort en peine, et ses espérances déçues l'ont jeté dans un état qui tient quelquefois de la fureur. . . ."

35. Ibid., XII, 220 - 21. To M. le Comte de Front, Saint-Petersburg, September 2, 1812: "Peu de batailles sont perdues physiquement . . . Les batailles se perdent presque toujours moralement; le véritable vainqueur comme le véritable vaincu, c'est celui qui croit l'être. Les bataillons qui avancent, savent-ils qu'il y a moins de morts de leur côté? Ceux qui reculent, savent-ils qu'ils en ont davantage? . . ."

36. Ibid., VII, 262. Report for His Majesty King Victor Emmanuel, October 8, 1812: "Ce n'est point une illusion; l'étoile de Bonaparte pâlit."

37. Ibid., XII, 280. Report for His Majesty King Victor Emmanuel, October 27, 1812: "Pour toute nation . . . la capitale est nécessairement un objet sacré, environné de grands souvenirs, et comme une espèce de creuset où s'elaborent toutes les idées nationales. . . . Moscou, dans ce genre, passait peut-être toutes les autres capitales. L'unité politique, l'unité religieuse résidaient dans ses murs. . . ."

38. Ibid., XII, 306. To M. le Comte de Front, Saint-Petersburg, November 10, 1812: "Je sortirais du style des relations et je prendrais celui de la poèsie, si j'entreprenais de décrire les cinq ou six premiers jours. Toutes les caves enfoncées à la fois; une innombrable quantité de brigands déchaînés et furieux, le sang coulant dans les rues avec le vin et l'eau de vie; les deux partis s'entr'égorgeant au milieu des flammes. . . ." aucune langue ne peut rendre ce spectacle ni même en approcher. . . ."

39. Ibid., XII, 424. A Mme de Constantin, his sister, Saint Petersburg,

April 25, 1814: "Je n'ai jamais cru un instant à la durée du *monstre* . . . mais je ne croyais pas du tout sa chute aussi prochaine. Il a eu au reste le plaisir de s'égorger lui-même; ainsi; le patient est précisément aussi noble que le bourreau. . . ."

40. Ibid., XII, 476. To M. le Vicomte de Bonald, Saint-Petersburg, December 1, 1814: "Je voudrais rendre à notre langue le sceptre de la philosophie rationnelle; mais le *commencement de la sagesse* en philosophie, c'est le mépris des idées anglaises. . . ."

41. Ibid., XII, 341. To Comte Rodolph, Saint-Petersburg, July 23, 1813: "Le morceau le plus remarquable de cet ouvrage qui a fait tant de bruit, est la *Profession de foi du vicaire savoyard;* ce qu'elle renferme de bon et de mauvais se trouve partout, mais non pas en si bon style. . . ."

42. Ibid., XII, 459 - 60. To His Excellency M. le Comte Jean Potocki, Saint-Petersburg, October 16, 1814: "Voila la mythologie chrétienne! C'est la vérité dramatique, qui a sa valeur et son effet indépendamment de la vérité littérale . . . tout le monde est peuple sur ce point, et je ne connais personne que l'instruction dramatique ne frappe plus que les belles maximes de morale et de métaphysique."

43. Ibid., XIII, 120. To Mme Swetchine, July 31, 1815: "La conversion est une *illumination soudaine.* . . . Nous avons une foule d'exemples de ce genre, même dans les hommes supérieurs les plus capables de raisonner . . . l'heureux changement s'opère subitement ou par secousses; toujours il commence par le coeur, où le syllogisme est étranger. . . ."

44. Ibid., XIII, 220. To M. le Comte de Vallaise, Saint-Petersburg, January 1816.

45. Ibid., XIII, 27. To M. le Comte de Bray, January 16, 1815: "L'Europe entière est dans une fermentation qui nous conduit à une révolution religieuse . . . dont la révolution politique dont nous avons été témoins ne fut que l'épouvantable préface. . . ."

46. Ibid., XIII, 156. To M. le Marquis Clermont Mont-Saint-Jean, September, 1815: "Si la palingénésie est possible . . . elle ne l'est que par l'Église. La Révolution française est satanique; si la contre-révolution n'est pas divine; elle est nulle. Mais où sont les éléments de cette contre-révolution? . . ."

47. Ibid., XIII, 189. To His Excellency Archbishop Severoli, December 1, 1815: "Dans le XIXe ils rétabliront l'Église pour raffermir leurs trônes, mis en l'air par les principes protestants."

48. Ibid., XIII, 50. To M. le Comte de Rossi, Saint-Petersburg, March 29, 1815: "La grande prétention de notre siècle est de se croire fort supérieur à tous les autres; et le fait est cependant qu'il est fort au-dessous; il est toujours en contradiction avec le bon sens ancien. . . ."

49. Ibid., XIII, 113. To M. le Comte de Vallaise, Saint-Petersburg, July 27, 1815: "Si le parti révolutionnaire se tire d'ici sain et sauf sans avoir rien perdu de tout le fruit de la Révolution, la partie de la Souveraineté est perdue. . . ."

50. Ibid., XIII, 168 - 69. To Prince Korlowski, Saint-Petersburg, October 12, 1815: "Mille raisons, trop longues à détailler, me prouvent que nous touchons à une révolution morale et religieuse, sans laquelle le chaos ne peut faire place à la création. La Providence se fait sentir visiblement. . . . Nous ne voyons encore rien, parce que jusqu'ici elle n'a fait que nettoyer la place; mais nos enfants s'écrieront, avec une respectueuse admiration, *Fecit nobis magna qui potens est.* . . ."

51. Ibid., XIII, 17. To M. le Comte de Vallaise, Saint-Petersburg, January 7, 1815: "Malheur à l'homme né dans un pays séparé qui va s'établir dans le pays dominant, où il n'a ni état, ni famille, ni propriété. Jamais il n'y prendra racine, il n'y sera que *posé,* comme on *pose* une assiette sur une table pour s'en servir un instant, et la renvoyer ensuite après l'avoir salie. . . ."

52. Ibid., XIII, 458. To Admiral Tchichagof, Saint-Petersburg, November 18, 1816: "Je ne sais . . . que le seul mot *khorocho,* indispensable à chaque instant pour louer tout ce qui se fait. . . ."

53. Ibid., XIV, 11. To M. le Chevalier de Saint-Réal, Saint-Petersburg, December 22, 1816: "Je me prosterne devant celui . . . qui a pu instruire, consoler, soulager ses semblables . . . ces héros de la charité silencieuse, qui se cachent et n'attendent rien dans ce monde. . . ."

54. Ibid., XIV, 148. To M. le Chevalier d'Olry, Turin, September 5, 1818: "Le mal est tel qu'il annonce évidemment une explosion divine. . . ."

55. Ibid., XIV, 246. To M. le Vicomte de Bonald, Turin, December 4, 1820: "J'ai rassemblé tous les signes (j'entends ceux qui sont à ma connaissance) qui annoncent quelque grand événement dans le cercle religieux. . . ."

56. Ibid., XIV, 139. To M. le Vicomte de Bonald, Turin, July 10, 1818: "Il faut être possédé de quatre ou cinq diables pour croire à l'invention des langues. . . ."

57. Ibid., XIV, 142. To Prince Korlowski, Turin, August 20, 1818: "Une impertinente femmelette, qui ne comprend pas une des questions qu'elle traite. . . ."

58. Ibid., XIV, 159. To M. le Vicomte de Bonald, Turin, March 22, 1819: Je ne sais pas si j'aurais été aussi sage, car peu de livres m'impatientent autant que ceux de Madame de Staël. . . . Quel dommage que cette femme n'ait pas été sujette spirituelle de la souveraineté légitime! . . ."

59. Ibid., XIV, 241 - 42. To M. de Syon, Turin, November 14, 1820: "Vous dites que l'Éternel *créa Chateaubriand pour guider l'univers.* On voit bien, excellent jeune homme, que vous avez dix-huit ans. . . ."

60. Ibid., XIV, 362. From Alphonse de Lamartine to J. de Maistre, Paris, March 17, 1820: "Vous avez fondé une école impérissable de haute philosophie et de politique chrétienne. . . ."

Chapter Seven

1. Mme de Staël, *Dix années d'exil, Oeuvres complètes* (Paris, 1904), VIII, 298: "Un désir russe, disait un homme supérieur, ferait sauter une ville."

2. C. A. de Sainte-Beuve, *Portraits littéraires* (Paris, n.d.), II, 42 D: "Trois écrivains du plus grand renom débutaient . . . au même moment . . . sous l'impulsion excitante de la Révolution française. . . ."

3. Ibid., II, 42.

4. Ibid., II, 448: "Les *Soirées* sont le plus beau livre de M. de Maistre, le plus durable, celui qui s'adresse à la classe la plus nombreuse de lecteurs libres et intelligents. . . . Chez lui, l'imagination et la couleur au sein d'une haute pensée rendent à jamais présents les éternels problèmes. . . ."

5. See my *Lamartine*.

6. *Cours familier de littérature* (Paris, 1859), VIII, *Entretien XLIII*, 44: "Tel est ce livre . . . un style étonnant de vigueur et de souplesse, des vues neuves, profondes, incommensurables d'étendue sur les législations, sur les dogmes, sur les mystères, et quelquefois des plaisanteries déplacées en matière grave . . . un *Diderot* déclamateur dans un philosophe chrétien et sincère. . . ."

7. Alfred de Vigny, *Stello* (Paris, 1882), p. 176: "Il a fallu à l'impitoyable sophistiqueur souffler, comme un alchimiste patient, sur la poussière des premiers livres, sur les cendres des premiers docteurs, sur la poudre des bûchers indiens, et des repas anthropophages, pour en faire sortir l'étincelle incendiaire de la fatale idée. . . ."

8. *Selected Journalism from the English Reviews by Stendhal*, ed. Geoffrey Strickland (London, 1959), p. 276.

9. *Mémoires de Sanson*, ed. Conard, Oeuvres diverses (Paris, n.d.), I, 219: "La Révolution a passé, et des abîmes où elle est descendue il n'est pas sorti une méditation immense. L'abus le plus large n'a pas été suffisant pour démontrer l'atrocté de l'usage; la peine de mort n'a pas été abolie . . . la loi demande encore des sacrifices humains. . . ."

10. Henri Gouhier, *La Jeunesse d'Auguste Comte et la formation du positivisme; Auguste Comte et Saint-Simon* (Paris, 1941), pp. 334 - 35.

11. Pierre Ballanche, *Essai de palingénésie sociale*, Oeuvres (Paris, 1830), III, 292: "L'Homme des doctrines anciennes, le prophète du passé . . . que l'on voudrait en vain ressusciter."

12. Edmond Schérer, *Mélanges de Critiques religieuses* (Paris, 1860), VIII, 294-95: "Que dirait-il . . . en s'apercevant que le centre de gravité du monde s'est déplacé et que la civilisation moderne est essentiellement une civilisation protestante? . . ."

13. Ernest Renan, *L'Avenir de la science* (Paris, 1890), p. 62: "Joseph de Maistre, un grand seigneur impatient des lentes discussions de la philosophie. Pour Dieu! une décision et que ce soit fini! vraie ou fausse, n'importe. L'essentiel est que je sois en repos. . . ."

14. Émile Faguet, *Politiques et moralistes du XIXᵉ siècle* (Paris, 1891), pp. 53, 56, 59: "Trés souvent en lisant les *Soirées*, on croit lire *Candide*. . . . On peut lire deux à trois cents pages de lui et le prendre pour un athée. . . . Je reste étonné devant ce christianisme où je ne trouve pas le Christ lui-même. . . . Jésus pour lui est une victime sanglante et rien de plus."

15. Ernest Psichari, *L'Appel des armes* (Paris, 1946), pp. 33 - 34: "Ce qu'il

lui fallait alors c'était une pensée catholique. Il allait à Pascal ou à Joseph de Maistre. Tout naturellement, il se tournait vers ces belles tiges droites, sans branches adventices ni nodosités, et où toute la sève se précipite vers le ciel, jaillit, verticale, de la terre vers le zénith. Voilà la seule beauté qui lui convenait."

16. Léon Bloy, *Le Mendiant ingrat* (Paris, 1928), p. 37: "La France n'est pas une nation comme les autres; c'est la seule *dont Dieu ait besoin*, a dit de Maistre, qui fut quelquefois prophète. Il y aura toujours en elle, quoi qu'on fasse, un principe de vie souveraine que rien ne saurait détruire."

17. Paul Bourget, *Pages de critique et de doctrine* (Paris, 1912), p. 264.

18. Charles Maurras, *Dictionnaire politique et critique* (Paris, 1932), III, 14: "Cet esprit juste qui, voyant avec une lucidité impitoyable les plus tristes, les plus dures lois de la vie, se faisait un devoir de confesser ce qu'il voyait ainsi qu'il le voyait, n'avait pas le coeur dur. . . . Il laissait la ferocité, même la dureté aux *idylliques massacreurs* de la Révolution, les Saint-Just et les Robespierre. . . ."

19. Albert Camus, *The Rebel*, trans. Anthony Bower (New York, 1954), p. 163.

20. See Bernard de Vaulx, *Joseph de Maistre* (Paris, 1940); Baron Michaud, "En relisant Joseph de Maistre," *Revue des deux mondes* (September, 1943, Vol. 80 or LXXX, 210 - 18; Stanislas Fumet, *Cahiers du Rhône* (Neuchâtel, 1943).

21. Among the works treating the influence of Maistre on Baudelaire are the following: J. Crépet, *Charles Baudelaire* (Paris, 1938); Daniel Vouga, *Baudelaire et Joseph de Maistre* (Paris, 1957); Mother Mary Alphonsus, *The Influence of Joseph de Maistre on Baudelaire* (Bryn Mawr, Pennsylvania, 1943); J. Massin, *Baudelaire* (Paris, 1945); B. Fondane, *Baudelaire et l'expérience du gouffre* (Paris, 1947); G. Blin, *Baudelaire* (Paris, 1948); Jean Paul Sartre, *Baudelaire* (Paris, 1947). Sartre's penetrating analysis of the Maistre-Baudelaire relationship merits the attention of students and researchers on the subject.

22. C. Baudelaire, *Histoires extraordinaires par Edgar Poe*, ed. J. Crépet (Paris, 1932), p. ix: "Quelle odeur de magasin!"

23. C. Baudelaire, *Correspondance*, ed. Y. G. Le Dantec (Paris, 1933), I, 130 - 31: "Qu'est-ce que c'est que l'homme *naturellement* bon? . . . L'homme naturellement bon serait un monstre. . . . Toutes les hérésies auxquelles je faisais allusion tout à l'heure ne sont après tout que la conséquence de la grande hérésie moderne . . . je veux dire; la suppression de l'idée du péché originel."

24. *Oeuvres de Baudelaire* (Paris, 1933), II, 637, 638, 640: "Quoi de plus absurde que le Progrés? . . . le Progrès aura si bien atrophié en nous toute la partie spirituelle, que rien, parmi les rêveries, sanguinaires, sacrilèges ou anti-naturelles des utopistes, ne pourra être comparé à ses résultats positifs."

25. *Les Fleurs du mal*, ed. J. Crépet (Paris, 1922), 327, 328: "Depuis le commencement de la poésie, tous les volumes de poésie sont ainsi faits. Mais

il était impossible de faire autrement un livre destiné à représenter *l'agita-tion de l'esprit dans le mal. . . .*"

26. *Ouevres de Baudelaire,* II, 649 - 51: "Les abolisseurs d'âmes *(matérialistes)* sont nécessairement des abolisseurs d'*enfer;* ils y sont, à coup sûr, *intéressés. . . .* La Sand est pour *le Dieu des bons gens . . . Le Diable et George Sand.*"

27. Ibid., II, 651: "Je m'ennuie en France, surtout parce que tout le monde y ressemble à Voltaire." "Voltaire plaisante sur cette âme im-mortelle."

28. Ibid., II, 629, 635: "La prière est réservoir de force. . . . Il y a dans la prière une opération magique. La prière est une des grandes forces de la dynamique intellectuelle. Il y a là comme une récurrence électrique."

29. Ibid., II, 648: "La peine de mort est le résultat d'une idée mystique, totalement incomprise aujourd'hui. La peine de mort n'a pas pour but de *sauver* la société, matériellement du moins. Elle a pour but de *sauver* (spirituellement) la société et le coupable. Pour que le sacrifice soit parfait, il faut qu'il ait assentiment et joie, de la part de la victime."

30. Ibid., II, 648: "Il n'y a de gouvernement raisonnable et assuré que l'aristocratique."

31. Ibid., II, 644: "Il y a dans tout changement quelque chose d'infame et d'agréable à la fois, quelque chose qui tient de l'infidélité et du déménagement. Cela suffit à expliquer la Révolution française."

32. Ibid., I, 23.

> La Nature est un temple où de vivants piliers
> Laissent parfois sortir de confuses paroles;
> L'homme y passe à travers des forêts de symboles
> Qui l'observent avec des regards familiers.

Selected Bibliography

BIBLIOGRAPHY

TALVART, HECTOR ET Place, JOSEPH. *Bibliographie des auteurs modernes de langue française (1801 - 1962)*. Paris: Editions de la Chronique des lettres françaises, 1928 - 1962.

THIÈME, HUGO PAUL, *Bibliographie de la littérature française de 1800 à 1930*. Paris: Droz, 1933.

For recent studies quarterly bibliographies of *La Revue d'histoire littéraire de la France* (RHLF) and *La Revue de la littérature comparée* may be consulted as well as the annual bibliographies of PMLA.

PRIMARY SOURCES

1. Editions (As yet there is no truly complete and definitive edition of Maistre's writings. Sources given below provide the student with available material essential to acquire a working knowledge of Maistre.)

Les Carnets du Comte Joseph de Maistre. Edited by Xavier de Maistre. Lyon: Vitte, 1923.

Les Considerations sur la France. Edited by R. Johannet et F. Vermale. Paris: Vrin, 1936.

Des Constitutions politiques et des autres institutions. Edited by Robert Triomphe. Strasbourg: Université de Strasbourg, 1959.

Correspondance diplomatique, 1811 - 1817. Edited by Albert Blanc. 2 vols. Paris: Librairie Nouvelle, 1860.

La Franc-Maçonnerie: mémoire au duc de Brunswick. Edited by Emile Dermenghem. Paris: Rieder, 1925.

Lettres et opuscules inédits. Edited by Rodolphe de Maistre. 2 vols. Paris: Vaton, 1851.

Mémoires politiques et correspondance diplomatique. Edited by Albert Blanc. Paris: Librairie Nouvelle, 1858.

Mémoire sur l'union de la Savoie à la Suisse, 1795. Edited by Robert Triomphe. Strasbourg, Université de Strasbourg, 1961.

Oeuvres complètes. 14 vols. Lyon: Vitte, 1884 - 1893. (Later editions identical.)
Du Pape. Edited by Jacques Lovie et Joannès Chetail. Génève: Droz, 1966.

2. Translations

Essay on the generative principle of political constitutions. Translated Anonymously. Boston: Little and Brown, 1847.
On God and Society: Essay on the Generative Principle of Political Constitutions and other Human Institutions. Translated by Elisha Greifer and Lawrence M. Porter. Chicago: Regnery, 1959.

SECONDARY SOURCES

BAYLE, FRANCIS. *Les Idées politiques de Joseph de Maistre.* Paris: Editions Domat Montchrétien, 1945. Lucid exposition of key points in Maistre's political philosophy.

DERMENGHEM, EMILE. *Joseph de Maistre, mystique.* Paris: La Colombe, 1946. Important analysis of theosophic influences on Maistre.

DESCOSTES, FRANÇOIS. *Joseph de Maistre avant la Révolution.* 2 vols. Paris: Picard, 1893. Penetrating examination of Maistre's career prior to Revolution.

————. *Joseph de Maistre pendant la Révolution.* Tours: Mame, 1895. A continuation of Descostes' excellent study tracing Maistre's career through the Révolution.

GOYAU, GEORGES. *La pensée religieuse de Joseph de Maistre.* Paris: Perrin, 1921. Old but useful study of Maistre's religious thought.

HOLDSWORTH, FREDERIC. *Joseph de Maistre et l'Angleterre.* Paris: Champion, 1935. Significant work on Maistre's knowledge of and contacts with English writers and thinkers.

LATREILLE, CAMILLE. *Joseph de Maistre et la Papauté.* Paris: Hachette, 1906. Thorough analysis of *Du Pape* and background of composition and publication.

LE BRUN, RICHARD A. *Throne and Altar.* Ottawa: University of Ottawa, 1965. Handy recent study of Maistre's political and religious thought.

TRIOMPHE, ROBERT. *Joseph de Maistre.* Genève: Droz, 1968. Detailed and conscientious analysis of Maistre's life and work.

VULLIAUD, PAUL. *Joseph de Maistre, franc-maçon.* Paris: Librairie Critique Émile-Nourry, 1926. Rather thorough treatment of Maistre's association with Freemasonry.

Index

155